Joe and the CEO

A Common Sense Approach to Changing Your Mind

Dr. Bob DeYoung

authorHOUSE®

AuthorHouse™
1663 Liberty Drive, Suite 200
Bloomington, IN 47403
www.authorhouse.com
Phone: 1-800-839-8640

First published by AuthorHouse 2/12/2009

ISBN: 978-1-4389-5648-0 (sc)

Printed in the United States of America
Bloomington, Indiana

This book is printed on acid-free paper.

Acknowledgements

I would like to acknowledge the following people, without whom this book would have never been in your hands today: Karin Singer, who not only helped edit this book, but who edited my doctoral dissertation, and occasionally edits Dave as well; Al D'Alessio, my 'Snopes' guy, faithful friend, and one of the most intelligent (and anal retentive) people I know; Dr Richard Maizell, who never tires of my 'right wing ramblings,' the Boboloanians—my 'dysfunctional family', and perhaps some of the most courageous individuals I have ever known. The thousands of clients I have had the privilege of treating throughout the years, providing me with real-life examples of proof that anyone can *change* if they want it badly enough; Don "Popeye" Mireau, a 78 year old personal trainer and friend, who never ceases to amaze me; and, finally, my best friend and loving wife, Stacy, who has encouraged me for years (sort of like 'nagging') to write down the 'quirky ways' I come up with things that express the gift God has given me to touch lives. Thank You.

Contents

Introduction

Dear Dr. Bob,

I just wanted to take a minute to let you know what I am thankful for…you.

My anxiety over holidays was well deserved as they started out a complete and total disaster…and then it was a Christmas miracle. Beginning Christmas with a fight with my father, which lead him to leave for a while, it made me see so many things…and then I didn't want to pretend or be quiet anymore. SO, with all the knowledge you have given me and some of the healing we have done, I told my mom why I was so angry at her, then I unleashed at my dad…and we all (minus my sister, who didn't show up) had the most EMOTIONAL day ever…and we all finally said things that we have never said to each other. It was amazing. We all cried, we all hugged, and although my parents still have a HUGE hole in their marriage and many of our relationships, I told them they needed to keep their problems to themselves; I no longer wanted to be the parent and would no longer be one.

My brother also said some things (FINALLY!) and it was great. You would have been so proud of me… I played you; my parents wonder if I am in the wrong field now! LOL…but before we closed it up, I said we all needed an action plan…

But my point is that, without you none of this would be possible…and my entire family talks about you...not only have you left a huge impression on my life, but you also managed to touch and gain the respect of a very hard, hurt man...and because of that, EVERYONE... is demanding to have you in their life as well!

So, from the bottom of my heart, I wanted to say thank you. Thank you for helping me get through this, keep me from going off the deep end (at least for a long period!) and leading me and my family on a path to healing.

Really looking forward to therapy next week!!!! Oh, wait, I am bringing the family....it's time.

With so much love and respect,

K. F.

Have you ever been so frustrated that you threw up your hands, berating yourself wondering why you 'do the same things over and over again, expecting different results', or do you believe change like K.F.s' is possible? Do you know people who are simply miserable most of their lives, but who wouldn't have it any other way? Do you really know what '*Healthy*' is? There are countless individuals out there who seem to moan about their fate, and complain endlessly, but who, nevertheless, wouldn't change a thing. Is it your impression that counselors or therapists are basically all the same—'head nodders' who are pretty much just as screwed up as the clients they work with? Have you gotten to the point in life where you are so frustrated with yourself and others, that you're coming to believe that change, *real change*, isn't even possible? So many people question *why* they do what they do, but does that type of questioning actually ever get them anywhere?

I have been in the field of counseling since 1978, working with more situations and presenting problems than most people could ever imagine. "You can't make this stuff up," would be a frequent saying throughout the years; and yet, I have had the opportunity of seeing hundreds of lives *change* for the better. I have seen what works, and what doesn't; and I have developed strategies over the years that evolved from trial and error, successes and failures. From the field of Forensic Psychology, inpatient mental health, emergency room crisis interventions, outpatient mental health, through inpatient, outpatient and intensive day program Addictions Counseling, Hypnotherapy, Biofeedback, work as an Interventionist, Trainer, Marriage and Family Therapist and Supervisor, up through being a nationally recognized lecturer, Police Academy Instructor and College Professor, I have just about 'seen it all'. There have emerged, through all this, certain *understandings*, truths, techniques and strategies that have proven particularly effective with the vast majority of problems people face. After developing them and using these successfully throughout the years, I finally decided to encapsulate them in this brief, easy to read book. I attempt to 'cut off the fat' and the chapters are intentionally brief and 'to-the-point'. Of course everybody has a 'unique' story, with details only they contend with, but the principles found here will, hopefully, be universal enough to apply to you and *make a difference.* 'Common sense', which apparently is not too common anymore, can still be called upon when it is put to work for you in a useable form; and *that* is a goal of this book. In addition to my background in Psychology, I have had the unique opportunity of being a Police Officer (actually a Motorcycle Cop) in Warwick, New York; perhaps one of the only officers in the country to be both a doctor and a motor cop...go figure. Experiencing 'Life" from so many perspectives, both 'on the street' and in the office, has promoted my shoot-from-the-hip (pun intended) approach that so many people appreciate; and that is what I put down in words for you in this book.

Change is possible—I see it happen every day.

Why We Don't Change

We are creatures of habit. How many people do you know who are miserable everyday but who would not change a thing in their life simply because it is what they are used to? They endlessly complain about not having enough money, bad habits, being fat or lonely, depressed, anxious, or just plain stuck in their self-imposed prison. Day after day, it's the same old routine and excuses: "I don't have the time," or, "I don't have the energy," or, "I don't have the money," or, "it's because of my family," or, "nobody understands me," and they just keep on with the same lame reasons over and over again. Miserable people only seem to love miserable company; and so it goes as the endless cycle repeats until they divorce again, get sick again, and complain their way through a life that seems to just pass them by with the 'wouldas-couldas-and shouldas.' When it really comes down to it, how many of our problems are self-imposed? It is as if we insist on paying some toll to get across a bridge, but we keep on backing up to pay the toll again and again without ever actually going over. Some "life script" plays itself out

> **Get honest** for a moment. What resolutions or promises have you made to yourself or others throughout the years? Jot a few of them down. How many of them did you make good on so far?

endlessly in our brain as we stay stuck and fed-up with ourselves. Are you one of these people?

One of the reasons we play out an often unwanted life script has to do with our neural structure. To illustrate: Most of my life I have been an avid motorcyclist. Anyone familiar with trail riding knows that, with time and repetition, a trail develops ruts that become tough to negotiate. The more a rut is travelled, especially during muddy conditions, the deeper it gets. After awhile, it becomes virtually impossible to steer the front wheel out of the rut; it naturally just slips in the ever deepening groove whenever you ride that trail; sound familiar? Thanks to technological advances, such as the electron microscope, we now know that learning actually elicits a *physical* change within our brains. As the ruts on a well worn trail deepen with use, so the neurons within the brain become modified. A process called "arborization" (deriving from the French word describing trees) occurs in which the synaptic gap between particular neurons decreases or increases with use. The neural endings (axon terminals) become more abundant when a habit is reinforced, so there is an actual physical change in our brains (called 'plasticity') as we repeat a behavior or thought over time. Thus the statement, "you can't teach an old dog new tricks" becomes more meaningful. If you wanted to create a new trail, it would initially be a real *Pain*. After hacking through dense brush to clear a way, there is the problem of forcing the front wheel of the motorcycle out of the rut, over the berm, toward the proposed new route; initially, it takes sweat, effort and commitment—*Desire*. This analogy fits nicely, but let's turn our attention to a frequently cited bugaboo of change.

The *unconscious* can potentially wreak havoc in our lives. Let me explain that our unconscious mind (you know, that part that seems responsible for a lot for the stupid things we do) is constantly taking in bits of information. If the average American actually does watch five hours of TV per day, I can only imagine what has become 'programmed' into our unconscious. Distorted images, misinformation and downright irrational propaganda can unfortunately become part of our network of 'reality' as well as inspiration, healthy desires and goals. Events from childhood, mistakes we've made, lectures given by our parents, or near-tragic situations in which we just barely got by, are all carefully tagged and stored by our unconscious for possible future use— it never stops working. We are continuously programming ourselves with whatever we choose to dwell on in our lives. That same old unconscious dynamic that gives you an "AHA" during the course of a day when you weren't really thinking about that song you previously tried in vain to remember, is partially responsible for some of the patterns we endlessly repeat and keep us stuck. Think of an aqueduct of information constantly flowing just beneath our awareness. As ground water inevitably seeps down, so do the tidbits of new information we acquire daily. The truth is that, with time, we can read, watch, listen, and talk about many things in our lives as we often try to make sense of our reality; this all permeates down, along with all the other stuff, and flows along with the unconscious material which *can* eventually influence us in any number of ways. The powerful unconscious is a force to be reckoned with; it usually takes the responsibility when we do the same stupid things over and over again—"I did it *unconsciously!*"

The only thing that takes more of a blame for staying stuck than the villainous unconscious is our propensity to default to "a chemical imbalance." "Pop-a-pill", infomercial mentality is all around us. If I hear of another person diagnosed as Bi-Polar, I'm going to scream! Either there is a virtual epidemic of Bi-Polars out there, or it's simply that insurance companies are reimbursing more easily for that particular diagnosis these days—good grief! Every professional in the mental health field is familiar with insurance driven treatment. By the way, it's amazing how patients miraculously recover when their insurance runs out. I'm not saying that there are not people with legitimate medical or genetic predispositions, but it has to be viewed as a continuum. There appears to be a pervasive willingness to defer *any* responsibility for change to something we allegedly have no control over. Unfortunately many psychiatrists, who often come across as omniscient and god-like, feed our belief that any problem we may be having is ultimately due to a chemical imbalance, and it is only a question of time until we find it. Colleagues have frequently joked that some psychiatrists appear to view any troubles as "drug depletion", and you can be sure that you will always walk away from their office with psychotropic medication regardless of the presenting problem—it's what they do. Can anyone honestly tell me they have consulted with a psychiatrist and have *not* been prescribed drugs? Being an informed consumer may convince you to take a good, hard look at the evidence before you run to the medication 'solution' too soon. Literature such as Dr Peter Breggens' book, *Medication Madness,* may open your eyes to the real 'cost' of going the medication route before you have explored the other options open to you.

Another frequent excuse given for failure to change, not unlike "failure to launch', is the blame our parents *must* accept for our misery and despair. Freud might turn over in his grave, but I just cannot, in good conscience, support the idea that, because your mother or father might have been lousy at parenting, you are simply a product of your dysfunctional home environment. It was just the way you were raised— accept it. Let's face it, I have never met a parent who, rubbing his or her hands, stated, "Oh boy, let me see if I can really screw this kid up." And there is a big difference between taking a look back at your past in order to reassess some things with 20/20 hindsight, and constantly dwelling on your lost youth with regret, blame and despair. It's not that I don't care if your mother didn't love you enough. If there happens to be a big issue that, for some reason, comes to the surface during the course of treatment, I always thought it more cost-effective to: *Trace it-face it-embrace it-and erase it.* People who continually live in the past, and harp on the mistakes of their equally dysfunctional parents, find themselves stuck in a quagmire that long-term, do-nothing therapists simply love; ineffective therapists call that job security. You may get insight out the wazoo, but you won't change a thing.

And now a word to the "WHYs." If I had a dime for every person who claimed, "Doctor—if I only knew *WHY,* I would change it." Nonsense! Most people who see me already know more about why they do what they do than I will ever know. I had a woman once who tenaciously clung to the idea that, if she only knew why she kept dating abusive or neglectful men, she simply would not do it anymore. Despite my best efforts to direct her otherwise, I finally gave in to her dogged determination to find out why. I told her that, look, because she was the first born in an abusive home with a father who was a 'King Baby", she was likely assigned the role of caretaker—junior mom. In family therapy terms, she would be defined as being "a parentified child." In Al-Anon terms she would be seen as a flaming co-dependent. She most certainly developed a sense of worth in fixing dysfunctional, needy people, and, as a result, would be "out of a job" should she ever happen to get involved with a more independent, healthy guy; she would find him boring. Darn if that wasn't her life story to a tee. After I was done, I asked her," Now, does that help you or make any difference?" She predictably replied, "No." I rested my case. Alcoholics in particular really love to pick therapists who make the mistake of getting into the WHYs of their drinking. I lost my job; I got a job; It's a nasty day; It's a nice day; My wife left me; My wife didn't leave me, etc., etc, while they gain all kinds if insight, they keep on drinking or drugging their life away—get the picture? They drink because they are alcoholic; the issue is stopping and staying stopped.

You do not have to keep playing the same old stuck-in-a-rut 'life script', blaming your parents and your past, spending thousands in therapy to find out "why." You can change your mind; and chances are you won't have to 'pop-a-pill' to do it! Positron emission tomography (PET scan) is a technological breakthrough that has revolutionized our understanding of the brain. The PET scan provides a computer-generated image of brain activity based on glucose consumption. This remarkable technique places detectors around the head that send data to a computer in the form of an actual moving, color picture. Incredibly, PET scans are so specific that they can tell us what part of the brain areas are being used when you are, for example, hearing a word, reading a word, saying a word, or even thinking about the meaning of a word. Case in point: Clinically depressed subjects show up on a PET scan as producing low activity levels in the frontal lobes of their brain. Following a four or five week trial of anti-depressant medication, they report feeling less depressed, and their scans show more activity and blood flow to that part which had previously been less active—Eureka! Proof positive that depression is caused by a chemical imbalance, and that's why I don't change—right? Wrong! I teach my psychology students a very basic truth about statistics: Correlation does not imply causation; that is, just because something accompanies something else, it does not mean that it *caused* it. What caused the alleged chemical imbalance in the first place, and, if there actually is a chemical imbalance, can only a drug fix it? Let's look at this from another view.

The same clinically depressed group of subjects was given PET scans, with the same indicators of low activity in the frontal lobes. Believe it or not, after they had participated in good cognitive-behavior therapy for roughly the same amount of time, without any drugs whatsoever, their PET scans revealed the very same changes in brain activity and blood flow! The mind-body connection can be truly profound. Did you know that Mark Twain was born when Haley's Comet came through? He predicted that he would die the day it came back-and he died the day it came back! If you have never read some of Norman Cousin's inspiring writings on the healing power of laughter, or *Healing Words* by Dr Larry Dossey, you are missing out. There is case after documented case of gutsy individuals who have turned what some physicians would say are hopeless and terminal situations around—or not! As an instructor in the Police Academy, I am aware of several cases of officers dying from gunshot wounds that were not fatal; that's right, they basically talked themselves into believing, "OH MY GOD—I'M SHOT AND I'M GOING TO DIE!"…and they do. Life is full of similar examples. Mind-body medicine is rapidly becoming one of the most popular and most promising professions. Thoughts can be responsible for the regulation of hormones, endorphins, serotonin, dopamine, and heaven knows what else. What used to be joked about and labeled by physicians as hokey now has an ever convincing body of hard research testifying to the credibility of the power of the mind, it's effect upon the immune system, the heart, recovery from cancer and many illnesses, and even life and death itself. When I was completing my master's degree at Montclair State many years ago, there was a couple down the street who were married since the Pope was an altar boy. They were obviously very much in love. One day the old fellow died unexpectedly. His wife of over fifty years, who was allegedly in perfect health, just lay down next to him, held his hand and died. Don't tell me that the mind doesn't have a profound effect on the body. Despite the fact that you may or may not have some legitimate medical malady, do not assume that it was necessarily caused by biology alone; and do not ever assume that only a biological intervention can correct it. Your attitude can not only keep you stuck—it can kill you. Make no mistake—your mind can absolutely change your chemistry!

Albert Einstein was obviously a great advocate of the power of the mind. Let me explain that Einstein believed that creativity is power, and that the *true* sign of intelligence is not necessarily knowledge, but *imagination*. A single creative thought can be one of the most powerful forces in the universe. With this in mind, I want you to believe in the power of your own creativity. This may be a strategic time in your life, with various circumstances leading you to pick up this book; or maybe you're *just ready*. Read this book *believing* that change *is* possible, and that it is possible *for you!* Every so often something comes along that makes a difference. Whether you call it a gift, a calling or simply that special connection that goes beyond words; I believe this book will touch your life in that way—if you let it!

This book is going to offer you solutions to your problems by finally allowing you to understand how your mind really works, and how to change it. People do not change because it is a good idea. I am convinced that we change—really change, only when it becomes too painful not to; and this becomes part of the following formula:

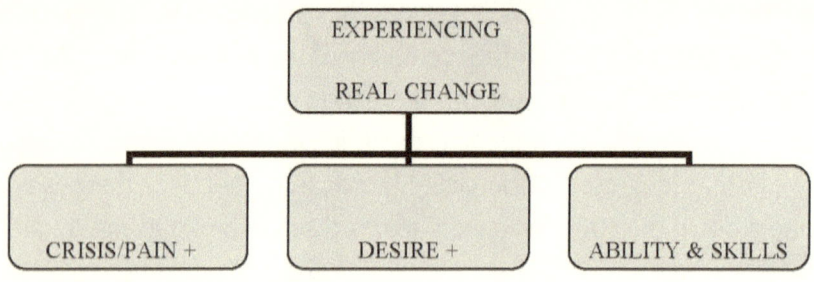

Nobody comes to me, or any therapist, because they're just so darn happy that they need to pay me a fee so they can tell me all about their joy. People only call me when their kid is angry, pregnant or on drugs, or their marriage is falling apart (I *am* cheaper than a lawyer), or because they're so depressed or anxious they can't take it anymore...or whatever—*not* because they're having such a great day. Think about the times when you brought about a change in your life; typically it initially involved physical and emotional *pain*. When a patient nonchalantly states, "Yea, I realize I'm an alcoholic...and I know I should stop drinking," I brace myself for the passive-aggressive game that will inevitably follow. This person has very little chance for any real change, despite the verbiage. They come to counseling because they are pressured by their spouse or their boss or the state; or maybe they want someone with a degree to scratch their itching ears while supplying lame excuses for them to continue playing the victim role. Working with someone like this is like fighting the wind—nothing to grab on to. People like this just love ineffective therapists who nod their heads as they talk about their feelings and endlessly go on about their mother or the terrible life circumstances they somehow endured—a complete waste of time and money. Give me a belligerent, nasty drunk any day that curses me out and calls me "YOU PEOPLE"; that is a patient closer to real change.

Any way you view it, there is inevitable, often gut wrenching pain preceding a significant change, but this means little without *Desire.* In the twelve-step programs[1] they call it "hitting bottom," being sick and tired of being sick and tired. It is possible, however, to 'raise your bottom,' thus increasing your desire or bringing about constructive pain that will motivate you.

In addition to *desire*, rarely does real change come about without some physical or emotional *pain*. Try to recall any real change in your life, whether a habit, a profound understanding ('aha'), or the acquisition of a skill; take a moment to remember and write down what it 'cost' you relevant to pain.

Using the formula above, you will be given the skills to change your mind. This book will target the *Whats* and the *Hows*—save the Whys for the head nodders.

How The Mind Works

I am going to review, step-by-step, the way you think because, after all, *as a man thinks—so is he.* Despite the fact that common sense is certainly not very common in America anymore, this chapter will break down your thought processes in a logical and absolutely common sense manner. When I'm done, it will be pretty hard to dispute the water-tight, practical understanding that I am going to give you. Getting a handle on this will allow you to begin mastering your thoughts so that you can finally, as my Dad says, "work smart—instead of working hard." ² Let's start out with the simple A-B-Cs, and later we will get to D.

Get honest for a moment. Are you ever aware of times when you talk to yourself? Even if it is not necessarily audible, everybody does it. Do you sound like a 'parent' disciplining someone? See if you can recognize and jot down a few 'choice phrases,' or put-downs that you use.

"A" stands for an activating event, something that starts the process. Imagine, for instance, that you're walking down the road on a beautiful day and, suddenly, a huge Rottweiler lunges out of the bushes for your leg! Now let's see, your senses kick in immediately and send information to that fabulous brain of yours. Your brain gathers the data, turns it into messages that can be understood, and it begins to go through a process not unlike the decision tree of a computer flow chart. Based on distinguishing features we can label this as "CANINE"—A BIG CANINE with BARED TEETH and FOAMING MOUTH! Your mind reviews past records, both personally experienced and seen in movies, and it determines possible outcomes—ALL BAD!

This wonderful brain of yours considers an action plan, releases the appropriate hormones, sends out the "fight-or-flight" commands to the sympathetic nervous system, and you JUMP AND SCREAM IN TERROR! Now, how long do you think that whole process takes—a millisecond? *That's* why they say that our brain is more sophisticated than the most advanced computer.

"B" is your *belief* or perception about the activating event. As in the previous example, we typically are not aware of our beliefs; they pretty much appear as automatic thoughts but they are always there; and these lead directly to "C"—your emotional *consequence*. To review: A—dog jumps out; B—big, bad canine is going to bite me; C—panic/excitement. You cannot have an emotional consequence without a preceding belief. Every emotion must have a belief that makes it so, and these beliefs come in the form of self talk. Someone once said that *all thought is nothing more than sub-vocal speech.* That is, we are constantly talking to ourselves, but we are usually unaware of it; it's at a sub-vocal level. They have even done experiments in which electrodes were placed on peoples' throats when they were thinking of something, and the electrodes vibrated. This understanding of subvocal speech has led to amazing research by a scientist by the name of Chuck Jorgensen, at the NASA Ames Research Center, utilizing technology to create a computer that can actually understand and interpret your thoughts based on reading subvocal speech. I discovered that, as we get upset, the *sub*-vocal often becomes *vocal*—"I can't belief this is happening…I must be an idiot!" Imagine if you were in a concentration camp. They deprive you of proper sleep and nutrition, and all day long there is a loud speaker blaring, "You stupid ass! You idiot! Loser! Just give up and die!" How do you think you'd feel after weeks of that? You would probably want to eat a bullet; and yet, this is the kind of stuff so many of us are telling ourselves every single day…all day long. This self talk kind of percolates, as I mentioned, down into our subconscious mind like ground water percolates down into the ground—down to the aqueduct. It can affect the brain chemistry. Eventually the ground water becomes saturated, and the water starts to bubble up over the top to create a flood; this is when people can experience anxiety attacks or depression—their beliefs, in the form of self talk, keep soaking down, down, down enough to saturate the 'ground' of their mind, and it simply bubbles over the top. That is why they often tell me, "I wasn't really *thinking* of anything. I was just watching TV (filling up those five hours no doubt) and out of the blue I had an anxiety attack—it has to be a chemical imbalance!"

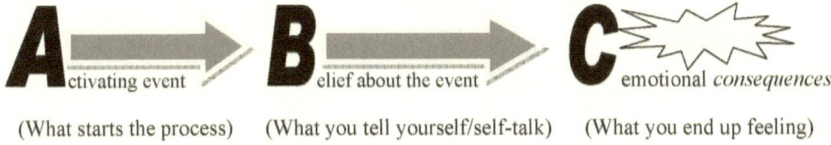

A ctivating event   **B** elief about the event   **C** emotional *consequences*

(What starts the process)   (What you tell yourself/self-talk)   (What you end up feeling)

Now imagine two babies on the beach. Neither of them ever experienced the ocean before, so neither has any prior learning to influence them. A big wave comes and knocks them down. One baby screams bloody murder, has a phobia for water and needs therapy for the rest of his life. The other baby screams with delight and wants to do it again; what's the difference?—their belief. Despite any genetic predispositions in temperament, which can go either way, it ultimately comes down to belief. What was 'A", the activating event?—the wave. The first baby, in his own baby way, says to himself, "life can be swept from me at any moment—and water is the culprit; be afraid—be very afraid!" The other baby sees that he is OK, gets excited and screams with delight—"gnarly wave dude!" He will probably be a surfer later on in life. Of course we shouldn't underestimate social referencing. This is when we pick up on cues from our environment to tell us how to act. For example, if an infant happens to fall down without really being hurt, she just gets up and continues playing—until she looks over at her parent gasping in horror! That's the cue to start crying and writhing in turmoil. Even on a pre-verbal, primitive level, infants engage in symbolic self talk. You simply cannot have an emotion "C" without a belief "B" causing it; there's always a belief, even if you are completely unaware of it—it's just how the mind works.

Let's look at another example. There are two guys in a traffic jam on the way to work, and they're not going anywhere. Both inevitably have the same consequences waiting for them at the end of the road...so to speak. One guy clenches his fist, lays on the horn yelling and cursing-road rage. The other guy applies the old serenity prayer, sits back and enjoys music on the radio-what's the difference between the two? "B"—their BELIEF! One guy carries on about how people suck and how terrible and awful everything is. The other guy accepts the things he cannot change and sees the traffic as an opportunity to listen to his favorite radio station. The activating event "A" is the traffic jam, but it has nothing to do with the driver's emotions—it is all about "B"—his belief, coming in the form of self talk.

I am going to show you now, beyond the shadow of a doubt, how even extremely powerful emotions are not only caused by our beliefs; they are defined by them as well. When I am done, a big light is going to click on in your brain, and you will be totally convinced. Are you a city person? I am not; as a matter of fact, the city is like a different country to me, and I only travel across the Hudson a few times a year for special events. Well, let's just assume that you're not really a city person but you decide to go to the San Gennaro festival in Little Italy with your goombahs. There are crowds of festive folks all around, and bouncy Italian music is pulsating through the streets—"Dut-dadada-Dut-dadada-dut-dadidility-da..." Suddenly you realize that you can't find your friends. You look around, up and down the crowded avenue, but they just aren't there. You think that, maybe, they went up another street, so you begin to walk that way. After awhile you realize that, not only are they not to be found—but you are lost. The street signs are missing, there's gang graffiti on the walls, and the overhead lights are blown out. In the city it can go from very nice to very nasty in a very short distance. Up ahead you see a bunch of unsavory characters that give you a real bad feeling. Against your better judgment you decide to quickly cut across the road and dart up an alley where you think you might hear some more activity on the other side. You begin to briskly walk up the alley toward civilization.

Right before you get onto the crowded street, a nasty looking big thug, wearing a black leather jacket and hoody, stops and turns in the alley toward you—and, you suddenly realize this is *not good.* You turn to go back and, right behind you, there are two big guys—one pulls out a switchblade! Get the picture? Put yourself right there for a moment. How does your breathing change? Think about it: It goes from low and slow (down low in your belly like babies or puppy dogs breathe when they're sleeping) to rapid and shallow. Your knees? They begin to shake; adrenaline and ACTH (natural rocket fuel) surge through them. I suppose this is when you hear stories about women picking up the back of a car that is on top of their child (of course they aren't able to walk for a week after that). Your hands? Cold and clammy. They are cold because the blood rushes from your extremities to the center of your body. God made our bodies so that we can maybe have an arm lopped off and still be able to run for a couple of blocks before bleeding out I guess. And of course they're sweaty to get rid of the heat you're producing. How about your swallow reflex? Think about it; it dries up, and you get cotton mouth. What do you think happens to your vision? If you put yourself in that situation, you realize that you get tunnel vision. You undoubtedly are not aware of the beautiful Greco-Roman architecture in the eaves above you. You do, however, see that knife clearly—like a magnifying glass focused in on the source of threat. Finally, what do you think happens to your hearing? You get tunnel *hearing;* that's right. You're not aware of the pigeon cooing up above, or the guy out on the street calling his son. You hear the click of the switchblade acutely, and even the squeak of his leather jacket.

You know, there is something called the "Cocktail Party"

phenomenon, the nature of which baffles scientists to this day. Imagine if you were at a crowded party with loud voices and activity all around—people speaking right at you. You suddenly notice that there's someone at the other end of the room trash-talking you! We cannot create a machine that can do this, but you can actually somehow filter out all of the voices and sounds coming at you, project over to the idiot over there saying ugly stuff about you, while our big mouths are still talking at you; and you can hear every word that he's saying—amazing! Well, that's what's going on in the alley—totally focused on whatever your mind deems a threat, and discarding anything else. Sort of like the Starship Enterprise after it gets hit by a photon torpedo. Just when the Klingons think they have them, Captain Kirk calls upon Scotty who re-directs the power, gives up warp speed, and puts up the rear shield again as he exclaims with his Scottish brogue, "That's all she can take Captain—she's gonna' BLOW, and we need more dilithium crystals!" Even Trekkies know that you have to give up something to get something, and that's what your body and senses are doing in flight-or-fight. So, let's review: Rapid, shallow breathing; shaky knees; cold, clammy hands; cotton mouth; tunnel vision; tunnel hearing; what do you call that, panic—anxiety? No. It's just neural excitement—nothing more. It is your *belief* that determines how it is perceived. "Wait," you may say, "panic is panic—there's no other way to look at it!" Oh really?

Change the scene completely. You are on your way home from an exhausting day of work. You decide to stop by your local convenience store to grab something cold to drink, and, while you're at it, you buy one of those scratch-off lottery tickets. At the counter you scratch off the first box on the ticket (you need three alike to win) and it shows three million dollars—yeah, you wish. You scratch off the second section and, surprise, three million dollars—In your dreams. You begin to scratch off the third section, and as you do, you start to see THREE MILLION DOLLARS appear! Suspended for a moment in disbelief everything takes on a kind of dream-like feeling until it actually hits you—you just won THREE MILLION DOLLARS—

THREE MILLON DOLLARS!!! How does your breathing change? That's right—rapid and shallow. Your knees?—shaky. What happens to the palms of your hands and your swallow reflex? You got it—cold and clammy; and cotton mouth. All you see is that ticket—tunnel vision; and you totally get in a zone. You're not aware of anything else going on in the store-tunnel hearing. You may even notice a time-distortion thing happens, when everything slows down, just as it did in the alley; everything seems as if it is in slow motion. So if I were in your body, monitoring what was going on, there would not be *one shred of difference* between being mugged and winning the lottery! The *only* difference determining whether the experience is perceived as excitement or terror is your *BELIEF*—what you tell yourself. Now does that give you a new perspective?

All our thoughts come to us in the form of 'sub-vocal speech', whether we are aware of them or not; the A-B-Cs of how our mind works is logical and easy to understand. Recall, and write down two contrasting situations, from your past, in which the actual feelings were similar but your interpretation of them (your belief) made a big difference to you.

3

Self Talk And Joe The Custodian[3]

Now that you are familiar with the "A-B-Cs", allow me to introduce you to "D"—disputing irrational and dysfunctional ideas; but first it is important to understand a very basic concept about habits. My swim coach once told me, "Robbie—you can't get rid of a habit." When I looked kind of baffled, he added,"…you can only replace it." I understood immediately what he meant. Try as hard as you can not to think about swallowing; yeah, the harder you try the more likely you are to swallow, right? I had a lady come into my office once, and when I asked her what she wanted to work on she replied, "Chocolate—I can't stop obsessing about chocolate. I can't stop thinking about the chocolate in my desk drawer at work; I can't stop thinking about the chocolate in the refrigerator at home; I can't stop thinking about the chocolate in my kitchen cabinet …""Stop!" I said, "What are you doing right now?" "Thinking about

> **Get honest** for a moment. Can you recall a circumstance when you were 'caught off guard' and something very unpleasant, and unexpected came your way? The entire day might have seemed to just fade away into darkness, as if a cloud overshadowed everything. Jot down, if you can, what it felt like, and how it affected the rest of your day..

chocolate," she replied. The worst thing you can do to get rid of a thought, or a habit, is to tell yourself, "Don't think about (whatever);" It is precisely the thing you do not want to do. The smart thing is to identify something when it does come along, and replace it. This should be a guiding principle as you begin to become more familiar with the irrational and dysfunctional self talk we are now going to discover.

There are several common dysfunctional ideas, going on in the form of self talk, that are very important for you to learn to identify and replace. Remember, ideas or beliefs ultimately dictate and possibly distort your reality. You will find that, as you get better at identifying these distortions, and gradually replace them with more realistic self talk, you will start to notice a difference. Taken as a shotgun approach, these will combine with other techniques that are going to bring about profound changes in how you think and how you feel.[4]

The first commonly held irrational idea is what we will call "**Dichotomous Thinking**;" that's a fancy term for when someone views everything as either black or white—all or nothing. It is important to install a dimmer switch instead of only having an "on" or "off." Let me explain: Is there any such thing as a good day or a bad day? "Oh yeah," you might say, "I've had a lot of bad days in my life." Really? How do you define a "day?" In my world, a day is defined as simply a 24-hour period—it is *neutral.* Now a lot can happen within that time frame. There can be some pleasant things and some not so pleasant things occurring throughout that day; but, no matter how you cut it; a day is a 24-hour period-nothing more. When you use sweeping generalizations such as "everybody," "nobody," "everything,""nothing," "always "or "never", you are engaging in the cognitive distortion of dichotomous thinking. By the way, *one of these days I really want to meet* EVERYBODY ELSES' MOTHER because she was constantly referenced by my kids as the ultimate litmus test for what should be allowed in the home (not to mention all that T.V. time she must have let all those other kids have). Just try complaining to an alcoholic that, "You're *always* drunk!" He'll quickly come back with the astute observation that, "Wait a second—there was a night last year, a Wednesday if I'm not mistaken, when I was definitely not drunk!" And you'll stand corrected. Dichotomous thinking over generalizes to the extent that it truly begins to twist your view of things, and your beliefs become increasingly distorted as a result. I will never suggest that everything should be just peachy-keen and wonderful. I just want you to be as realistic about life as possible. Realistic self talk leads to realistic and manageable emotions.

The next commonly held dysfunctional belief is that of "**Filtering.**" When someone stomps on your toe, you don't care that the rest of your body feels great; all you think about is that darn toe! If nine people say, "You're terrific—what a great person you are; what a pleasure it is to be around you—you're wonderful," and one person says, " You're an ass—I can't stand you," who do you listen to? Of course, you only hear that person who hates you, and the rest are filtered out. Here is a story that really clarifies this concept: A few years ago I bought the first new car I ever owned. It was a typical mid-life crisis sports car; a liquid silver convertible Toyota MR 2 with black interior, TRD racing suspension, mid-engine, and it drove like a go kart that was street legal—what a blast! That car took corners like a Formula one race car, and it looked as if it cost a lot more than it actually did. I only owned it for about two months prior to taking it up to Lake George with my wife. There was a conference at a resort up there where I was going to speak to various law enforcement professionals on the subject of occupational stress. When we pulled into the Village of Lake George and finally found a parking space, my wife opened the door into a garbage compactor and put a dent in it! Despite her futile attempts to console me and give me perspective, all I could see was a dent with a car around it. Naturally I just had to use that incident during my presentation, as a very real and personal example of filtering. The example was certainly fitting but, of course, I left myself open to cop humor for the rest of the weekend: "Nice car, Doc...except for the dent." After the conference was over we were in kind of a hurry to get home. I was cruising down the thruway at, shall I say, an excessive rate of speed. Now this car handled as if it was on rails—on a dry road. I hadn't yet driven this baby in the rain and, you guessed it, the sky opened up and it started coming down like cats and dogs. My honey (or should I say, 'my adult supervision?') spoke up and asked me to please slow down. Just as I responded with, "OK" (I didn't quite fully get the "K" part out) the car started to hydroplane. We started to spin around, and we launched down the middle of the highway and over the embankment. I repeatedly told her, "get down—get down," as the car slid over the edge, Frisbeed across a small river, spun into various bushes and trees, scraping, crunching and cracking until it came to an abrupt halt with a crash. As the mud and steam settled I looked over at her and asked if she was hurt; "No, I'm OK, "she said, "Are you alright?" "I'm fine," I responded. After a pregnant pause she then said, "You still mad about the dent?" We had a good laugh and suddenly the dent did not matter all that much anymore. Forcing yourself to gain perspective (seeing the big picture), *regardless of how it feels*, goes a long way to correct the distortion of filtering. Acknowledging *all* the data, whether the stuff that is pleasant or unpleasant, helps to more quickly regain a realistic appraisal of events; thus, any emotional consequences more quickly become realistic and manageable.

"**Catastrophizing**" (which is not really a word *yet* in the English language) is a by-product of our word inflation. Just as so many grades and educational degrees in America are being cheapened, so our vernacular is increasingly incorporating exaggerated and inflated terms. Let me explain: How many times do you hear people describe a song, or a car, or a print on a napkin as "awesome, or incredible?" "It's *totally unbelievable* that she would even *think* that," someone blithely says, "…just amazing!" Tweaked up language leads to tweaked up emotional consequences. When God returns in the clouds, or when a fifty-foot tsunami is about to engulf my house—*that's* awesome, not a napkin pattern.

What have you ever experienced in your life that is "horrible, terrible," or "awful?" We categorize the commute to New York as such, but it is exaggerated and inaccurate. I am not saying that there are not unfortunate people out there who have not been subjected to something awful, but, for Pete's sake, let's call a spade a spade. During the course of my career of over 20 years as a therapist I have worked with two people who have endured stranger abductions of their children—now *that's* truly horrible. The commute to New York is just a pain in the butt, not a torturous experience. Still not convinced? I have developed a macabre reality-orienting scale designed to give you instant perspective; I call it the "Body Parts Scale." Imagine a scale of 1 through 10 (AKA a Likert scale) in which a "1" is a really bad headache. A "2" would be a really bad tooth ache. "3" is a badly chipped tooth. A "4" would be if someone were to take bolt-cutters and clip off the pinky toe of your left foot (it gets worse, but stay with me). "5" would constitute someone taking those bolt-cutters and clipping off the pinky toes of both feet. "6" involves clipping off the big toe of your right foot. You guessed it, "7" means clipping off the big toes of both feet. Go to "8" and you are going to get the pinkies of both fingers removed (without anesthesia of course). "9" involves the loss of both pinkies as well as the thumb of your non-dominant hand. Make it to "10" and you will be losing both pinkies and both thumbs—get the picture? Now you tell me how far up the scale you would venture in order *not* to commute to New York; probably not even a "2,"—so don't tell me it's "horrible" or "terrible;" it is just, as I said, "a pain in the butt," and nothing more. Of course, if someone were to abduct my little girl, I would be willing to go to "10" in order to prevent it from happening, or to get her back, as I'm sure would most parents; that would accurately be described as "terrible." Exaggerated and unrealistic self talk, however, inevitably leads to exaggerated emotional consequences. It is important to keep that stuff in check. When you catch yourself describing things with unrealistic, exaggerated and tweaked up language, simply identify it and replace it with a *realistic* appraisal-*regardless of how it feels* at the time, and you will begin to reap the benefits of more balanced, manageable emotions. "Ah," you may say,"…but it *feels* like it's horrible." This is probably one of the most common forms of irrational and distorted self talk I come across; and this is what we address next.

"Emotional Reasoning" is probably the most common of all cognitive distortions. This irrational self talk comes in two versions—'regular' and 'premium.' Our culture and, unfortunately, our relationships are guided and dominated by emotions these days. The teens even have a sub-group dedicated to this very concept; they call themselves "Emos;" (They're probably the ones most likely to actually *appear* on T.V.). Nevertheless, this particular distortion takes the form of equating an emotional state with reality. For example, if I *feel* hopeless, does that necessarily mean I *am* hopeless?—of course not. If I feel like a freakin' alien, does that mean I *am* an alien?—obviously not. Feelings have very little to do with reality. The sometimes more subtle form of emotional reasoning comes in the form of confusing thoughts with emotions. For example, if I were to assert," I *feel* like you are an idiot," does that express a feeling or a thought? It is neither a thought nor a feeling; it's kind of a *thinky-feely* statement that tricks your mind into allowing an emotion into the door where only a thought should be. If you were to tell me," I *feel* like I'm no good at anything," I would probably ask you who dressed you today; you were obviously good at that. When it comes to getting a handle on this concept, I like to use the analogy of your mind being like a business with a large building. Down in the basement is Joe the Custodian. He's big and strong, but not necessarily the sharpest knife in the drawer, if you know what I mean. He represents your emotions, and his job is to stoke the furnace, keep the air conditioning going, and clean up once in awhile. He is important in keeping the business running, but he also needs to be kept in his place. Up in the penthouse suite, on the top floor, is the CEO with the MBA from Harvard. He, or she, is the brains of the operation. The CEO does the actuarial reports, keeps the business running from the top down, and represents your cognition—your higher-order thinking. Now late at night, Joe sneaks upstairs into the CEOs office, smokes his cigar with his feet up on the desk as he sighs, "I could get used to dis'-faggettaboutit." Suddenly, someone knocks on the door; Joe quickly gets his feet off the desk, and pretends he's cleaning up—*that's* what happens when you allow your emotions to run the show. Just imagine Joe doing the actuarials, deciding who gets raises and who doesn't, and developing future plans relevant to company mergers, etc. You might appreciate Joe's input as you would with any employee, but if you permit him to take over your business, you're going belly-up in a couple of weeks. Is it Joe the custodian or Joe the plumber running the White House nowadays? Either way, it would be equally wasteful to have your CEO stoking the furnace or sweeping up the floor. Each is important in running the business, but each must be kept in his or her place. Think about anytime you let your emotions "run the show," and I'll guarantee you behaved in, shall we say, a less than wise manner. Our prisons are full of people who allowed Joe to run their business. If I let my emotions take charge of my life, I'd probably be dead or in prison—get the picture?

The key is to gain skill in acknowledging what you are feeling at any particular moment (I'm not telling you to completely deny your emotions); but to simply allow the feelings to pass by as you engage your cognition—your problem-solving tool. Always defer to the CEO. Remember to act your way into feelings, as I said before; never allow yourself to *feel* your way into actions. Never put Joe in charge. I find it frequently helpful to condition myself to take a slow, deep breath prior to acting on any emotion (verbally or otherwise) in order to delay that automatic response for a couple of seconds; it has saved my tookus more than I can tell you. Throughout the years I have had the opportunity to testify in court as an expert witness many times. Lawyers love to pummel shrinks with yes-no questions, often completely out of context, in order to have the witness trip up by blurting out something that paints himself into a verbal corner. The slow, deep breath habit is invaluable prior to answering even the most elementary questions, providing you with a precious moment to think and sound professional.

On another practical level, the slow, deep breath routine has saved me some embarrassment. After becoming a motorcycle cop (one of my childhood dreams come true) I was barely on the job when, on a back road one evening, a perpetrator shot past me in the opposite direction. I whipped the cycle around and took off after him. Once he spotted me on his tail, he turned off his lights, blew right through two stop streets, and blasted onto the main road carelessly disregarding any traffic that may have been in his way. Of course most departments discourage high-speed pursuits, barring 'smoking gun' felons, but this guy was obviously running for a reason, so I just followed him due to his "failure to comply." When speeds rocket close to 100 miles per hour on back country roads one has a tendency to have that 'fight-or-flight" thing kick in (I know—just neural excitement). Eventually he realized that I was not going to let him get away-and there's no way he was going to out run my BMW KT 1200 Police Special! He finally pulled over underneath a street light, enabling me to call in his tags. Have you ever heard an officer call in something to the dispatch in the midst of a harrowing experience? It doesn't sound pretty. Lest I come across as an adolescent girl on the radio, I remembered to take that slow, deep breath first, and all was well.

This chapter would not be complete without a look at the "**Shoulds**." I am going to state something that, at first, will sound pretty dumb. The second time you hear it, it may sound more interesting; and by the third or fourth time, it might even come across as possibly profound. Here it goes: "Everything that has happened to you and me *should* have happened, because it *did*!" You might wonder what the heck I am talking about; let me explain. Neither you nor I, nor anyone I have ever met, have ever been able to change the past. We can certainly look back at the past and re-evaluate things that may or may not have happened, adding insight and learning from past events; but, unless you have invented a time machine that allows you to actually go back into the past to erase and replace past mistakes, everything that has happened, from this point back, *should* have happened because it *did* (if you *do* come across such technology, by the way, I am definitely *in*). It doesn't mean that what happened was good, or right, or pleasant; it simply means that it *happened*, and we cannot, no matter how hard we try, go back to re-do it. It *should* have happened because it *did*. When people continually gripe, "I *should* have said something; she *shouldn't* have done that; that *shouldn't* have happened," they are just, as my Mom would say, "…getting their knickers in a twist.' Albert Ellis has commented that these people are '*Shoulding all over themselves.*" It makes no sense at all to continually dwell on the past, with its regrets, mistakes and pain, when there is simply nothing that can be done about it.

If we are standing in line for about an hour to see a movie, and some stoonad cuts in front of us—*should* that have happened? Yes—because it did! That does not make it right, or fair, or pleasant-but there is absolutely nothing you nor I can do to make it *not* have happened. At that point I can choose to grumble under my breath. Or I could say, "Hey—Buddy, the line starts back there!" Or I could do a Rambo on him and choke him out; or I could get the manager to do his job; or I could simply ignore him and gripe to someone else about how people suck. Regardless of what I chose to do, however, I cannot make that not have happened. We are particularly vulnerable to the Shoulds following a crisis. How many parents have cried, "I shouldn't have let her go out that night—if only I had stopped her?" All this type of irrational self talk does is to further frustrate and depress them, because the truth is that it *should* have happened because it *did*. That doesn't mean that it was OK or that they won't grieve for many years to come. If my little girl goes out and gets plowed down by some drunk driver, should that have happened? Yes—because it did. That doesn't mean that I won't grieve for the rest of my life, and that doesn't in any way imply that it was right—it just happened, and it is up to me to do the best I can to turn it around for myself and others who love her. The Shoulds are left over from our infantile magical thinking days when we believed that, if we just wished hard enough, we could somehow change whatever went on. As an adult, it is time to identify the Shoulds and replace them with something that we can do something about. Being stuck in the past paralyzes us in the present. Consider our past mistakes as gold that, if we see them as such, can help us to really appreciate the cost of what has made us who we are today. There's a popular quote I often use: "It is what it is."

You might question, "How does this identification and replacement of distorted self talk get worked out in therapy?" Allow me to present a typical example: A woman who suffers from anxiety attacks comments, "I'm afraid of driving because I feel dizzy sometimes." I ask her to clearly map out her thoughts in a logical, flowchart manner. We go through a Socratic-like questioning routine: "OK, let's take a logical walk through the scenario that is leading up to your fear:

Q: "How often do you actually feel dizzy?

A: Sometimes twice or three times a day.

Q: And have you ever felt dizzy when you were driving?

A: Yes, twice.

A: Did it lead to an accident?

A: No.

Q: Is it dizziness that concerns you, or is it the fear that dizziness may lead to disorientation?

A: The second thing—disorientation.

Q: Has *that* ever happened to you when you were driving?

A: No—but it might.

Q: If it did, what are you afraid might happen?

A: I might crash.

Q: If you ever felt dizzy, as you have in the past when you weren't driving, would you, realistically, be able to pull over?

A: Probably—but maybe not if I was in the fast lane in heavy traffic.

Q: How often do you drive in the fast lane?

A: Once in awhile.

Q: Have you ever driven in the fast lane when you were afraid of getting dizzy?

A: No.

Q: So, assuming you might be afraid of being dizzy; you would most certainly drive in the slow lane where you would have plenty of time to pull over?

A: Yes."

This type of yes-no questioning, following a logical progression through reasonable outcomes and actions, usually goes a long way in allaying unreasonable fears. After awhile, the patient gets used to this method of logical progression through his or her thought processes, pointing out any irrational beliefs along the way, and they eventually internalize the process so well that their emotions inevitably become more realistic. This Socratic questioning is at the heart of Cognitive Behavior Therapy (CBT) which is very effective in keeping Joe in the basement—it works!

Imagine, on the other hand, a typical traditional therapy session with the same patient:

Q: "How do you feel?

A: Anxious. (long pause)

Q: What makes you feel anxious?

 A: Driving. (longer pause)...

Q: Uh huh, tell me more about this anxiety and driving.

A: Blah, blah, blah (free associations, and Mom inevitably comes into it).

Q: So you first felt this way around your mother?

A: Yes, Doctor...she was terrible, etc."

At this juncture the therapist encourages the patient to ramble on endlessly about his or her mother, real or imagined childhood experiences emerge with resulting tears and/or anger, and the patient leaves the session feeling much better (maybe) but still doesn't drive. There may be lots of insight but very little progress toward real change in the presenting problem. As I said, the WHYs do not seem to provide an effective access to change; the WHATs and HOWs, in my opinion, present much more fruitful possibilities.

As you review and become more familiar with the common cognitive distortions (beliefs) in your life, you will be surprised just how often you are buying into them. By identifying and replacing them with realistic self talk, and gaining skill at laying out a logical progression of your thoughts, you will begin to feel the difference; it will give you a leg up on bringing about some changes.

Our self-talk (beliefs) can typically come to us in the form of common cognitive distortions that can, in turn, profoundly affect our 'reality'. Copy the list of distortions, post them in an eye-catching place (like the refrigerator) and take time this week to see if you can identify and replace the ones you are currently using—the results might surprise you.

4

We Are Addictive By
Nature, So Harness It

A Viet Nam era cartoon character by the name of Pogo is often cited as proclaiming, "We have met the enemy and he is us." There is no getting around it—it is important to draw our attention now to the elephant in the living room, so to speak. The most fiercesome battles we will ever fight will not be engaged in the deserts of Iraq or the jungles of Panama (or the streets of Newark, New Jersey after hours for that matter), but they will be fought within our own hearts and minds. We are addicts by nature. Who cannot identify with the concept of "part of me does, and part of me doesn't" whenever we are trying to bring about a change? It is as if there are literally two people within us. Asian philosophy describes the ongoing tension between the Yin and the Yang. In the New Testament, the Apostle Paul writes, "For what I want to do I do not do…For I have desire to do what is good, but I cannot carry it out… For

Get honest for a moment. How many situations in your life can you remember when you were 'your own worst enemy?' Jot down a time when you knew something was unhealthy or just wrong, but you did it anyway. Reflect for a moment…Did shaming yourself really change anything?

what I do is not the good I want to do; no, the evil I do not want to do—this I keep on doing." (Rom 7:14-19). This chapter is going to approach *desire* from a different perspective.

I am going to give you a workable and practical definition of addiction—one that can apply to any addiction. One might see addiction as an extreme form of *desire*, but there are actually three criteria that must be satisfied in order to have a diagnosis: First; There must be *LOSS OF CONTROL* of either the 'usage" or the behavior around it. The old saying, "The man takes a drink—the drink takes a drink—the drink takes the man" could apply here, if one were addressing alcohol in particular. Drinking, for example, after you decided that you wouldn't, or drinking more than intended, is clear loss of control. If this were to be applied to sex, food, work, (TV?) or whatever, the criteria would be the same. There is also loss of control relevant to one's behavior *around* the addiction. There was a movie awhile back, entitled Shattered Spirits, in which Martin Sheen played the role of an alcoholic. I recall being pretty impressed by how realistic one scene depicted what AA would call "stinkin' thinkin'," or alcoholic loss of control. The family was in the van, waiting to leave for their vacation, when the father (who was not actually drunk at the time) noticed that the lawn was not mowed as he had asked. "I thought I told you to mow the damn lawn!" he yells, as the wife attempts in vain to do the Co-dependent shuffle and try to calm everyone down. "Now Honey," she pleads, "Don't *Honey* me!" he screams, as the kids start to cry, "I'll mow the *#@#* lawn myself!" At which time he proceeds to fire up the lawn mower, cursing and swearing, running over the rose bushes in a fit of anger and alcoholic loss of control, and they never end up going on vacation. You don't have to be intoxicated to exhibit an emotional loss of control around an addiction. Joe the custodian successfully initiates a coup whenever this happens.

The second criterion of addiction involves the fact that it *TAKES PRIORITY* in the life of the addict. Let's face it, if you asked any addict if their addiction 'takes priority', they would sarcastically respond, "... oh, yeah—it's *real* important." Denial ain't a river in Egypt. How can we tell if something actually does take priority in someone's life? Well, if I were to ask you what was very important in *your* life, what would you say? Your kids? Your job? How could I determine if something was a priority with you without actually asking you?—by simply observing you. I would see that you spent time, money and interest around that which you claim is a priority; in other words, you would be *preoccupied* with it. When I was in High School, anyone could tell that motorcycles were a priority in my life. I wore motorcycle T-shirts; carried around motorcycle magazines; hung out with other kids who were into motorcycles, and I spent every penny I had on my motorcycle—it was a priority. You will clearly see if something is a priority in your life, or the life of another, simply by observing; it's very simple to see a preoccupation. Remember that "Chocolate Lady" I spoke about earlier?

The third and final criterion of addiction is that the addict continues *USING DESPITE NEGATIVE CONSEQUENCES.* I suppose the adage "doing the same thing over and over again, expecting different results" would fit nicely here. If I were to ask the addict to list all the ways alcohol consumption has helped him and his family, there would likely be a long pause followed by a blank stare. If I were then to ask him to honestly list all the ways alcohol has hurt him and his family (assuming he was that in-touch) there would undoubtedly be a rather extensive and painful inventory; yet, the drinking continues anyway—despite negative consequences. "Doctor, it hurts when I do this!—then don't do that!"

Loss of control	+	Takes priority	+	"Use" despite negative consequences
(of your usage or behavior)		(Preoccupation)		("Doc, it hurts when I do this!")

Think about how well this definition fits with anything that can be considered an addiction. Let's take a look at over-eating in America, the fattest country in the world. Who wants to be fat? (Aside from Sumo wrestlers, as my son astutely pointed out)—nobody; and yet, an estimated 65% of us are. Why? That's right—you *know* why; you eat too much, you eat the wrong foods, or you don't get enough exercise, and the WHYs do not help you to change do they? You might engage in comfort eating. You may overeat to avoid intimacy. Perhaps you overeat simply because you conditioned yourself like Pavlov's dog. Whatever the reason, real or imagined, it comes down to somehow identifying and replacing that compulsion (desire) with something else that floats your boat in a healthier way if you want to change.

Co-dependency is another addiction that does not involve a "substance," per se; and yet it is every bit as deadly as any other addiction. The Co-dependent, usually a parentified child who grew up in a home that had addiction, mental illness, extreme religiosity or a parent with ongoing chronic sickness, finds worth only by fixing dysfunctional or irresponsible others. They do not know the difference between "caring" for someone and "caretaking;" the key being not to do the things that another person *could* and *should* be doing for themselves. The Co-dependent typically hooks up with someone who is needy, demanding, and usually not considered an 'equal' in many ways. This gives the Co-dependent a false sense of control and worth, not unlike that which they had as a child growing up. Sometimes outsiders wonder, "How the heck did she ever wind up with such a loser?" It reminds me of what a used car salesman once told me: "Doc," he said, "There's an ass for every seat."

Not only does Co-dependency help destroy the character of children subjected to it, it becomes an intrinsic component of an addicts' sick system in the form of enabling the sickness to progress. They actively prevent the addict from feeling the pain of their consequences, naturally occurring as a result of the addiction, by constantly stepping in to "save" and protect the addict. The addict is never allowed to "hit bottom," or the child under the Co-dependent's care is never allowed to learn responsibility for his or her actions by feeling the consequences (remember, pain is an essential component in the formula for change). The Co-dependent literally kills people with "kindness," and I use the term loosely.

When you think about it, the Co-dependent, who subtly wants to be seen as a martyr, is actually quite selfish. Their feelings of being liked, or not having to deal with the anger, displeasure or hurt of the object of their caretaking (their addiction), become more important to them than the actual well-being of others. One woman whom I just started to treat for her incredible Co-dependent behaviors, found herself, yet again, wanting to return back into 'the belly of the beast' by moving in with her drug addict, abusive boyfriend lest she feel responsible "for hurting him." As she began to understand what she was really doing, and started to bring about changes in her life, she exclaimed, "Wow—I almost let Joe the Custodian kick the #%&*#@#* out of the CEO!" The Co-dependent clearly exhibits *loss of control* around the object of their addiction; they become obsessed with what the other person is or is not doing, thus it *takes priority*; and the Co-dependent exemplifies 'doing the same thing over and over again, expecting different results,' thus displaying the third criterion of addiction: *"using" despite negative consequences.* Instead of a substance, the Co-dependent's addiction takes the form of another *person*, but they have the very same symptoms as any other addict. Co-dependents will typically display an ever increasing tolerance for the addicts' behavior over time, just like an alcoholics' increased tolerance for alcohol. What would have sent them running years ago now somehow becomes more acceptable. Interestingly enough, the Co-dependent will even experience 'withdrawal' symptoms in the event that he or she ever decides to cease their Co-dependent behaviors. When they stop enabling the addict, it is common for the Co-dependent to suffer from anxiety, insomnia, the shakes and a host of other physical symptoms not unlike those of a detoxing alcoholic—what do you think about that!? Learning to apply the serenity prayer, and to detach with love, as they teach in Al-Anon, may become a life-long pursuit of re-educating yourself. As the skills of re-directing that energy become honed, however, the Co-dependent can learn to live a fulfilled life while they "Live and let live." Without considering the *entire* formula for change, however, it is unlikely that the changes will endure.

Asians use ideograms in their writing; you know, they look a bit like pictures instead of the typical letters we use. Interestingly, the Chinese ideogram for "Crisis' has a double meaning that is fairly profound. The literal translation is: "Opportunity in the Midst of Crisis." Despite our tendency to dig our heels in when we become threatened, a crisis can present an open window, so to speak, for changing our minds; *that's* why the first part of the formula from chapter one inevitably involves a crisis (pain). That pull toward homeostasis (steady-state) can temporarily shift during a critical time in our life. I have successfully organized quite a few interventions in which family members literally overwhelm an alcoholic in denial with facts related to his or her drinking, thus intentionally throwing him into a crisis. This can often successfully "raise the bottom" of an addict. It is probably the most stressful therapeutic technique one can ever orchestrate—but it can be extremely effective. When you experience a crisis in your life, don't see it as "horrible, terrible," or "awful;" see it as an essential part of the formula—an opportunity in which a window of change is opening right in front of you. There is certainly some truth when people say, "When one door closes, another opens."

When I first participated in the martial arts many years ago, I was so impressed with a demonstration of the advantage of skill over strength. I watched a frail-looking little Japanese Sensei (Master) toss a huge guy around the room, as if he were made of balsa wood, simply by re-directing his weight. Anyone who has studied Aikido knows the amazing power of blending and re-directing an opponents' attack rather than doing the pedestrian thing of fighting muscle with muscle. The martial arts also teach you to take fear and redirect it into aggression. That energy has to go somewhere; why not direct it toward your adversary? What does this have to do with our propensity for addiction you might ask? I am going to introduce you now to the concept of developing a *positive addiction*. William Glasser, the developer of Reality Therapy and Choice Theory, wrote a book several years ago about positive addiction. Understanding this concept will enable you to blend and re-direct the potential opponent within.

As you review the three criteria for addiction, think about how you can begin incorporating small routines in your life that may, in some ways, reflect the addictive process in a positive way. Harness your natural propensity for your benefit. Routines can readily become positive addictions given the right training and mind-set. Just keep repeating whatever it is you wish to get "addicted" to, *regardless of how it feels initially,* and you will eventually open yourself up to the addictive process. My buddies in AA claim that, if a recovering person spent as much time in meetings as they did in the bar, they'd do just fine. Addicts go on and on about, "switching addictions." Certainly one of the most common positive addictions is discovered by many athletes in the form of "the runners' high." Endorphins (literally "the morphine within") eventually begin to kick in following a prolonged period of aerobic activity. If you are exercising to the extent of breathing heavily (not so much that you couldn't talk) and you are sweating, you are probably in that aerobic zone. The literature is jam-packed with scientific studies attesting to the mental and physical benefits of regular aerobic activity. I have seen people wean themselves from psychotropics, reduce their depression and anxiety, enhance their tolerance for pain, and remedy a plethora of physical complaints simply by developing a regular exercise routine. It is just so darn cost-effective. The trick is to not do too much at once—you don't want to overdose. Remember, "a little done a lot is better than a lot done a little." Give me someone who incorporates a 10-15 minute brisk walking routine daily any day over a nut who busts his keister in the gym for three hours one day and then never goes back. If you are feeling a little anxious and antsy when you haven't worked out for a couple of days—that's good. When you start to schedule your life around an exercise routine or buy a house within proximity of a gym—that's good. You may notice a slight preoccupation with exercise developing; toy with it; don't overdo it or you'll scare off your sub-conscious. Gradually turn those routines into positive addictions. The litmus test should be whether or not the "addiction" is ultimately beneficial to your mind and body, or not; invite the 'symptoms.' Consistently pairing-up *any* behavior or thought with something positive and/or pleasurable creates a Pavlovian conditioning potentially leading to the addictive process.

Understanding our mind relevant to our addictive nature can enable us to reap many benefits for change. Here is another concept, born of the addiction, that can be harnessed: "Euphoric recall" is a term I use frequently to describe the distorted way addicts "remember" events when they are under the influence; it is one of several reasons why they don't "get it" when assessing their own drinking problems. When an alcoholic is intoxicated, the alcohol drastically influences how they perceive reality. Their honest belief is that they are the life of the party when, in fact, their spouses or friends are feeling humiliated and embarrassed by the alcoholic's inappropriate shenanigans. Their "beer muscles" encourage thoughts of grandeur and skill; and it makes their date seem increasingly more attractive as the evening progresses (or should I say, "regresses?"). The "high" developed by being three sheets to the wind distorts their reasoning abilities dramatically, and, in retrospect, the addict only seems to "recall" that high (euphoric) feeling while being totally unaware of the shame, frustration, fear and anxiety his actions created in those around him. "People *love* me when I'm drunk," they say, having no clue what people really think-until the day after. Many Co-dependents, who had sworn that they had enough, and that they were "going to finally leave the bum," inevitably find themselves victims of euphoric recall as well. "He wasn't *that* bad," they proclaim, "...and nobody understands him the way I do." All of a sudden, they only seem to remember the fun times and the flowers. Such an incredibly potent distortion of reality! The question becomes, how do you harness this aspect of addiction to make euphoric recall work for you?

We are going to delve into the power of imagery more later, but it becomes relevant now when considering the use of euphoric recall for your benefit. One of the most amazing things about the mind is that it transcends space and time, and sometimes reality. With the proper incentive we can imagine virtually anything we want. Prior to relapse, addicts creatively *only dwell on images and feelings of euphoria* relevant to the upside of their usage. They carefully select what they will drum up, and it usually skillfully eliminates the episodes of hugging the porcelain god, if ya' know what I mean. They effectively distort their reality to the extent that they only recall the euphoria—the rush. If addicts can so easily conjure up euphoric images and feelings while excluding the downside of their addiction, why can't you? As I am about to end a workout session, I intentionally see and feel myself enjoying the run, or whatever I am doing. It only takes a moment, prior to concluding, to relax and envision yourself as strong, poised and ready for more—*regardless of how it feels.* I have conditioned myself to custom-make my images to motivate and inspire me, and so can you. Remember the analogy of developing that new trail? It may take some effort in the beginning, but, with time and practice, you can gain some real skill in using that amazing imagination of yours. Develop your images and empower your thoughts and feelings about activities you want to strengthen. "What the mind can conceive—the body can achieve!"

> The tendency to acquire addictions is in our nature, and loss of control, being preocccupied, and doing it despite negative consequences defines it for us. Recall and write down a time in your life when you felt physical or emotional discomfort that resulted in discontinuing something *positive*, and if you can see it in terms of an addiction; now come up with something that you would *want* to be 'addicted to'.

5

Normal Versus Healthy

"**W**hy can't you just act normal?" my parents would say as I was growing up, and I chuckle when I sometimes see that popular bumper sticker: WHY BE NORMAL? My psychology students at the State University of New York are quite familiar with the difference between normal and healthy. I teach them that "normal" is a statistical average, a mathematical formula for determining a central tendency of a particular population. You may not remember an old T.V. commercial (yeah, it regrettably must have influenced my life too) about prunes and constipation. The actor said something along the lines of, "Prunes…is one enough—are three too many?" A commentator would then enter the scene with the statement, "Doctors say 'normal is what's normal *for you*," and the commercial would make a pitch for some laxative. I remember joking, "Yeah, so if I'm a serial killer, it's just *normal* to mutilate bodies and bury them under my porch, because it's normal for *me*." What is deemed "normal" for any group of people at any

> **Get honest** for a moment. Jot down something in your past that would have been a better, healthier choice for you, but you did something else just to 'keep the peace' or fit in. What did doing what others consider to be 'normal', instead of what would have been healthy, 'cost' you?

given time may be a far cry from "healthy." Think about what may have been normal for the general population of Nazi Germany during the height of the Third Reich. I will probably never aspire to being normal, even if it were possible. Being healthy, on the other hand, might prove to be a worthwhile endeavor. Anyone truly interested in changing some things has to at least have an idea of what it is to be healthy. My students know that, unlike "normal," "healthy" addresses a quality of life issue.

Allow me to present you with a succinct, and perhaps oversimplified, lesson in abnormal psychology. After we are born, life can be good. If our parents provide a predictable, nurturing and secure home environment, we can accept life on life's terms—it's *all* good. If, on the other hand, life kind of sucks because our parents are nuts and the home is stressful and unstable, we have the propensity to distort reality in order for it to become more palatable; this distortion of reality is called a "neurosis." Freud would say that most of us are neurotic. Maybe that is because most of our parents *are* nuts (or maybe it's just all that darn T.V. influence), but we will find that which can be learned can be *un*learned. Nevertheless, if our home life turns out to be *so* bad that as infants we simply cannot make any sense of life, we will create our *own* reality; this is called a "psychosis." With that in mind, we can explore our psyches in comparison to what many people consider the *real* 'crazies' out there. R. D. Laing, by the way, was of the opinion that many psychotic individuals were, for the most part, the ones who were probably the *most realistic* individuals in our insane society! I'm not sure if I can argue with him about that. Of course there *are* some individuals who clearly display a biological predisposition, or who have suffered an organic trauma, thus rendering them impaired. The nature v. nurture (biological v. environmental) debate has raged on for decades with both sides providing persuasive points. I would not overlook or minimize unfortunate people who were dealt a legitimate 'biological blow;' I'm simply providing you with an alternative paradigm for understanding *some* crazy, over the edge, thinking or behaviors we may come across. It also gives us a model to work with *prior* to running immediately to psychotropic medication.

I believe that people whom we consider insane could be presenting the same behaviors and thoughts that every one of us displays almost daily; they only exhibit them to *more* of an *extreme*. How many of you would not be looking over your shoulder following an act or situation that makes you feel guilty? You know what they say: "Just because you think people are out to get you, doesn't necessarily mean they are not." Paranoids do just *that* to more of an extreme. How many of us wouldn't "go postal" in the event that we were watching the playoffs, and the TV goes blank right before the possible touchdown play upsetting the game? (Would that be considered TV withdrawal symptoms?) The Obsessive-Compulsive individual feels just the same way, frustrated and overwhelmed, whenever he or she becomes thwarted in the middle of a routine. Our quirky idiosyncrasies and symptoms are nothing more than a continuum, the ends of which are more clearly seen as "disturbed", but the center comprises the stuff that individuality is made of. If you are rich, I suppose your nutty symptoms would be labeled as "eccentric," but if you're poor, I guess you'd be classified as JPN (Just Plain Nuts). Being diagnosed with a mental illness comes down to very limited criteria: (a) Do they (the symptoms) cause you significant personal upset? (b) Do they significantly impact upon you occupationally—are they a real problem with your job? And, (c) Do the symptoms really screw up your social life? You have to be able to come up with a resounding "YES" on all three counts in order to qualify with a legitimate diagnosis. Keep in mind, however, that the Diagnostic and Statistical Manual of the Mental Disorders (DSM), which is used by almost all therapists, is the end result of a bunch of clinicians getting together to agree upon clusters of symptoms that they categorized to make sense of dysfunctional thoughts and behaviors in people. It's possible that they ultimately wrote the DSM to get insurance money for the work they do.

Why Be Normal?

It is sometimes very difficult to determine if someone is off the deep end. We can be anything we want to anybody, when we are cool calm and collected. Healthy folks, who just happen to be experiencing an unusual and overwhelming amount of life stress can *appear* to be really disturbed. Really disturbed individuals, on the other hand, can seem to have it all together if their life happens to lack any real stressors these days. To the uninformed outsider the two are easily misinterpreted. Ultimately, people are like hydraulic systems. A hydraulic system utilizes fluid under pressure that can be harnessed to develop incredible power. Emergency workers have been able to save countless lives with the aid of the "Jaws of Life," a hydraulically operated scissor-like machine that can literally rip open metal in order to gain access to trapped accident victims. It is the weak point of a hydraulic device, however, that will blow when the pressure gets too great. We all have weak points (whether genetic or environmentally determined) and, with enough pressure, we too will 'blow.' *The true test of mental health comes down to the capacity of each one of us for*

enduring stress or pressure on our 'system.' Some people are clearly on the edge; they will beat you up if you just look at them the wrong way. I shudder to think about all the 'live wires' there are running around in our society. Some people are running on empty, ready to 'blow' any minute. When enough pressure gets applied to your system, you will see your 'weak part.' Some will drink alcoholically; some will become clinically depressed, or develop an anxiety disorder. There are individuals out there who have a tremendous capacity for stress on their system—but everyone inevitably gets confronted with their breaking point sooner or later.

When I was a kid and my new brother arrived, my Grandmother came over from England. She actually came over for a visit—and stayed for 21 years! "Nanna" and I never really got along all that well (she doted over my little brother) and, unfortunately, I would sometimes do things to 'get her goat.' Now, I seemed to be completely resistant to poison ivy back then. One day my buddies and I were outside in the yard, sweating and running around. Nanna yelled out the window, "Watch out you don't get poison ivy!" Of course I felt compelled to show off by breaking off a big, fuzzy branch of that infamous plant, and I proceeded to rub it all over my face in order to state my case. You guessed it—my naturally terrific immune system was shocked and it became overwhelmed. The next day I looked like Alvin, of 'Alvin and the Chipmunks', and through barely opened eyes, I apologized for being such a brat. The analogy here is that, despite our natural capacity to endure stressful situations, we all have those points in our lives when our coping system becomes overwhelmed and we break down; it's not *if,* it's *when.*

The "normal" ebb and flow of stress in our lives is to be expected. I constantly remind my patients of a very important adage dealing with the inevitable stressors in our lives. It revolves around the fact that, as I said, we *all* have times when we go down. Everybody has down time when they feel hopeless, discouraged and possibly overwhelmed; but for those times I tell them, "*It's how far down you go, and how long you stay there.*" This is a measure of normal versus healthy. The addictive process within us, as mentioned, tries to throw us in to the dichotomous, all-or-nothing mode during down times; "Well, I *blew* it now—might as well go all the way!" The alcoholic rationalizes many a bender with this irrational self talk. "OOPs, I slipped and had a drink," he bemoans, "…so I might as well drink the whole case!" The chronic over-eater eats a cookie, or varies from the typically unreasonable diet plan he/she has set up, and thus the inevitable feeding frenzy ensues with, "Oh well, I blew it now-might as well 'enjoy ' it…let's gobble up the entire box!" That makes about as much sense as saying, "I stubbed my toe—might as well just cut it off." Resiliency, the ability to adapt and overcome, is surely *the* cornerstone of mental health as well as intelligence. A slow, deep breath to interfere with the automatic, trance-like state that results in this thinking, can be followed by a call to a sponsor, immediate removal from the situation, rigorous exercise, going in to another room to listen to a relaxation tape, etc, all allowing you to not go down *as far* or stay there *as long*.

Unfortunately few people actually prepare for the inevitable 'down time'. I tell people that soldiers do not build sandbags during a firefight. It is impossible to be filling and stacking bags of sand while enemy bullets are flying past your head. The time to prep for the fight is *before* the first shot is fired. As you continue in this book, you will be able to custom make strategies and techniques that will be effective *for you* in your battle against the inner enemy *before* you are overwhelmed by another defeat of the "Poor-Me's." You already know *WHY* you do most of the things you do. You already know what your button pushers are, if you think about them. The challenge gradually presents itself as one of developing a game plan that is effective so that you don't go down as far, and you don't stay as long. Your quality of life will be enhanced and your ability to bounce back more quickly will be fortified—and *that's* what ultimately defines "healthy."

With this in mind, can you arrange to develop a clearer picture of yourself as resilient, adaptive, pragmatic and happy? Do you have an idea of what a healthy person thinks and feels and does on a daily basis? If you have ever experienced the joy of a job well-done, you have a hint of "healthy." If you have ever disciplined yourself to endure for a cause, to overcome the desire for immediate gratification in order to secure a bigger reward, you have a hint at "healthy." If you apply the lessons of this book in your life, such as never letting 'Joe the Custodian' (your emotions) rule your major decisions, *regardless of how it feels,* you will get a hint at "healthy." Overall, 'healthy', like *happiness,* is a quality of life that comes as a *result* of correct thinking—not vice-versa. And, as I said, your mind and your body are intertwined with each profoundly affecting the other. Once you start to become more healthy, that healthy outcome will serve as a foundation for increasingly more healthy decision-making in your future…and happiness will come to you as the inevitable by-product. We will delve into the secret of happiness in detail at the end of this book; for now, however, I want you to begin developing an understanding, an idea of just what "healthy" is so that you can incorporate it when you target change in your life. Remember, "Normal" has little to do with it.

'Normal' is a statistical average, and 'healthy is a quality of life; aside from the impact certain things might have on your functioning (positive or negative) your concept of 'healthy' can be defined by how far down you allow life's problems to take you, and how long you stay there. Take a moment to write down what, specifically, *you* would envision as a 'healthy' person, in relationships, work and lifestyle; how do you realistically compare?

6

Arguing Well

If you have a heartbeat and an opinion, you are going to argue. In addition to this wonderfully obvious point, is the fact that you are not alone in this world. Whether you like it or not, all of us are destined, to a greater or lesser extent, to need others and to inevitably interact with them (unless, of course, you spend your entire life in front of the TV). With this in mind, it is time to present eight simple rules of good arguing—a time for building skills. These rules apply to couples, families and parents, so you are going to get more bang for your buck. Before I present them, however, it is important to note that you have to view them in a realistic light. The extent to which you use these rules, when you get into disagreements, is the extent to which you become a better communicator; that is, do not view them as "working" or "not working" in your influence of others. If you are saying, "I tried 'I-statements,' and they don't work," you are not getting the idea. It is not whether or not they *work* for getting the desired

> **Get honest** *for a moment. Take a look back at some 'arguments' you have had. Do you recall the arguments themselves, but not what you actually argued about? How many times did you really change the opinions or lives of others, or have them change yours, by yelling louder, and getting more emotional?*

responses from others at the time, but rather, it is the understanding that, to the extent to which you use them, *you* are becoming a better communicator—whether you get the desired response from whomever you are talking to or not. By the way, if you do use these rules, you are more likely to be heard and understood anyway, and that is going to go a long way in working on yourself and influencing others for bringing about changes. The Old Testament states, "As iron sharpens iron, so does one brother sharpen another," (Prov. 27:17) and I try to view every 'disagreement' as just another growth opportunity. These are the basic guidelines, the peddle and gas if you would, for learning how to drive down the road of change relevant to interacting with others in your life.

RULE ONE: *Use 'I' statements instead of 'you' statements.*

This first rule may sound a bit superficial but, just like the 'Shoulds" it can have a profound impact if you understand it and use it effectively. An 'I' statement does two things: First, it forces you to be accountable for yourself, and only yourself; secondly, it allows you to express yourself in a manner that is most likely to be heard. Few things will turn someone off more quickly than a statement starting out with "YOU (fill in the blank)." When people hear the 'you' part they are already composing a defensive response, and, because of divided attention, that means they are really not listening to anything else you have to say—it's human nature. After the 'you' they hear you as if you were Charlie Brown's parents; remember them? They would speak in the background to Charlie and his friends, and all you would hear is, "Mwaa, babaa, maw-maw-maw." A good 'I' statement has two parts: The first part is a *feeling* not a thought. Even if you start out with "I feel…" it does not necessarily mean you are using a feeling; for example, if I say, "I *feel* like you're an idiot," I am obviously not using a feeling. This statement is actually an example of Emotional Reasoning, previously mentioned, in which that *thinky-feely* thing happens—not a feeling or a thought. If you are saying "I feel *like,* or I feel *that* (fill in the blank)" you are not using a feeling at all. "I feel angry," or "I feel relieved," or "I feel hurt," are examples of feelings—not "I feel like (fill in the blank)." Do not allow Joe the Custodian to have access to the CEO's office by giving him permission to masquerade as a thought. The second part of a good 'I' statement is an *objective, specific, factual* observation—not an opinion. "I feel angry when you act like a complete idiot," is neither factual nor specific nor objective, and you will not be heard. "I feel angry when I'm talking to you and you walk away from me," is much better. "I feel _____ when you _____," is the foundation of a proper 'I' statement, although the order can be switched. When I say, "Nathanael, I feel frustrated when I asked you twice to pick up your shoes and they're still in the hallway," that turns out to be a pretty nice 'I' statement. Of course he could respond by blaming his brother, saying, "Ben put them there!" He certainly cannot argue that I do not *feel angry,* nor can he rationally debate my objective observation about the shoes. A good 'I' statement, well placed, can be extremely effective; and whether or not it gets the response you are looking for, it just makes you a better communicator when you become proficient at it. It may take a little practice, but it's well worth it.

RULE TWO: *No rhetorical questions.*

A rhetorical question is one that has no answer, such as, "How many times do I have to tell you?!" A long time ago (I emphasize that for a reason), I was a lot less mature than I am now (If you can believe that). Some guy was tailgating me while my buddy, my five year old son, and I were driving early one morning to play tennis. I foolishly 'brake-checked' the guy in order to teach him a lesson about driving too close. Much to my surprise, he skidded off the road and the front of his car looked as if it was stuck in a ditch. I slowed down to make sure he was alright-which he was. My buddy exclaimed, "What did you do *THAT* for?!" I explained that the idiot should learn to drive defensively—which did not exactly go over well. As we proceeded I watched in my rearview mirror as he rocked his car back and forth until he dislodged his front end from the ditch. At this point I commented to my buddy that, "It looks like we're in for a little road rage," as I saw the guy speed toward us (Joe the Custodian should never drive). By the way, I only had a ratty Ford Pinto and he had a Pontiac Firebird, so there was no chance of escaping my fate. The guy proceeded to catch up and overtake us, but instead of passing us (maybe while flipping us the bird) he pulled up alongside us. With his window rolled down, and obviously in a state of rage (thus the term), he began yelling obscenities while gesturing for us to, "PULL THE #@%&*%#* OVER!" An interesting bit of family trivia that applies here is that, in my family, we have a tendency to laugh when we are nervous, which doesn't exactly help when someone is totally pissed at you. Naturally I was scared, so I began laughing, which only served to infuriate the driver all the more. He pulled his car back behind us as we turned off the main road toward the tennis courts behind the High School. "I sure hope your Karate works," my bud nervously commented, "because this guy looks really big and nasty!" I asked him to watch my son, and I would take care of the situation as best I can. We pulled into the parking spot by the courts and, sure enough, the road-rager positioned his car directly behind ours—preventing any chance of escape. As I walked out into the lot, he jumped out of his car and ran toward me. Now this guy had bigger biceps than my legs, and he had no neck! My mind raced with options—all bad, as he closed the gap screaming obscenities and flailing his arms. Just before he entered what the Japanese call 'my-eye,' striking distance, I put up my hands and said, "Stop!"—and he *did*. With that, he proceeded to use the 'F' word at a rate heretofore never imagined. Finally, after he was 'F'ed out, he said in a voice not unlike Lenny in Steinbeck's classic novel, "Why are you so F-in' STUPID?!" I thought for a moment, and then responded, "Sir, I don't know whether it's environmental or genetic." He was clearly stumped. The point is that he used a rhetorical question—it had no answer! A well placed 'I' statement would have been so much more effective. Imagine how much better it would have been if he said in his 'Lenny voice', "I *feel* angry and scared when I'm tailgating you, and you slam on da' brakes." I guess I would've apologized at that point, and we'd be playing tennis. Joe *hates* when that happens!

RULE THREE: *No flooding.*

Flooding occurs when you allow yourself to get so angry or upset, that you become overwhelmed and act like a tantruming child in an adult body (sort of like the fellow in the story I just told). This is when you invite Joe the Custodian to successfully initiate a hostile takeover of the entire company. Think of two arrows, one going up and one going down:

The more emotional you become, the more likely you are to act in a primitive, infantile manner. You can be anything you want to anybody when you are cool, calm and collected; but when the 'Do-Do' hits the fan we tend to act in a hard-wired way. It's almost impossible to turn it around once you're flooding, so the trick is to re-direct it *before* you flood. When I speak with patients about their knock-down, drag-out meltdowns, they typically remember the incident, but, surprisingly, they usually do not remember what they were flooding about in the first place. Needless to say, you cannot get rid of a habit; as I mentioned before, you can only replace it. The *no flooding* rule involves three steps listed above: You first say, "I'm flooding," or some other statement *identifying* that you are flooding; it's also helpful to agree upon a sign or symbol of some kind (I lift up my hands, but some folks prefer the 'time out' symbol). You then leave the situation, maybe go outside, and relax with that slow, deep breath. When you have sufficiently 'chilled,' you come back. If your spouse, or whomever you are arguing with, allows you to leave, you have to come back within a reasonable amount of time (maybe 10-15 minutes), or you would be punishing your partner for giving you the time and space. When you use the *no flooding* rule, it is important to have an understanding that you are not to be followed while you are leaving (no trailers). It is also important to remember that you cannot tell another person that *they* are flooding; if they don't get it, *you* simply say, "I'M FLOODING!", whether you actually are flooding or not—and *you* leave the room; the outcome is the same. This rule works like a charm. Just remember that your words are sort of like a tube of toothpaste; once you put the toothpaste out there on your finger, you can't get it back in the tube. Once you say emotionally charged, destructive things, you cannot take them back. Just as James wrote in the Bible, "...the tongue is a small part, but it makes great boasts...the tongue also is a fire, a world of evil among the parts of the body" (James 3:5-6). The *no flooding* rule, when used in a timely fashion, can save you a world of grief, and it can help bring about some practical changes in how you manage to keep Joe in the basement at crucial times.

RULE FOUR: *Respect.*

I have never, in all my years in this profession, heard of someone being disrespectful and degrading to someone else, and getting a positive response. People can say the most demeaning and obscene things when they are angry. I have seen couples literally *spit* at each other during an argument, and I certainly have heard worse. Now tell me, have you ever cursed out and degraded a loved one, only to get an understanding and mature response such as, "Well, now that you called me a #@%^^&$*ing Son-of-a-_____, I'm so much more willing to hear what you have to say." That's why Joe the Custodian should not be in charge of the company's public relations; never let those emotions do your speaking. Maybe in your family arguing or anger was never safe. I find that families that "never" argue are very similar to those who seem to argue abusively—neither is "safe" when it comes to the expression of anger. So where would you learn how to express yourself in this way? You are not going to learn from those five hours a day of TV; nor are you going to have a relationship in which you will never become angry—not if you enjoy any type of intimacy. ANGER HAPPENS, but I don't need to call others foul names. If I'm really angry, I can simply use an 'I' statement—" I'm *REALLY* angry...REALLY, REALLY angry!" If I am too angry, there is always the *no flooding* rule. Regardless of what you were taught in your family of origin, everybody gets angry, but it does not need to be expressed violently or disrespectfully. Do not mistake raising your voice upon occasion with being disrespectful. Say what you mean, mean what you say—don't say it mean.

RULE FIVE: No laundry lists.

Have you ever known couples or family members who, every time they get in an argument, pull out 'the list'? "Back in 1904 you said about my mother (fill in the blank)!" They seem to receive some bogus power from meticulously keeping a tally of anything and everything you or others have ever done wrong. By the way, how many times has the list of wrongs proven to be an effective change agent?—NEVER! But, as I said in the first chapter, we are creatures of habit even in the face of obvious stupidity. We just seem to keep doing the same old things over and over again expecting different results. If it happened *yesterday* that's one thing; but if it happened years ago, and if it's already been discussed ad nauseum—for Pete's sake, LET IT GO AND GET OVER IT! My Dad told me that, whenever you point a finger at someone, you have three of your fingers pointing back at you.

RULE SIX: Sandwich it.

What is a sandwich? It would be described as two pieces of bread with something in the middle. This rule reflects a common technique of 'positive-negative-positive' taught in supervision. Instead of blasting someone with criticism right away, it may help a little to start off with something positive (the slice of bread) such as, "I've noticed that you've been really trying to control your temper lately—and I appreciate it." Then comes the 'meat'... "But yelling at me when I first walk in the door, just makes me feel more defensive and on edge." This is followed by another piece of bread (positive); "I do want you to know, though, that I appreciate your effort to listen." It may sound somewhat contrived, as do most things that are different, but you will get a lot more mileage with it, and, who knows, you just might end up being heard.

RULE SEVEN: *Listen first, and then give your side.*

If I had a psychotic patient in my office, exclaiming that he was the illegitimate son of Mary Magdalene, and that the CIA was tracking his thoughts, etc., the *last* thing I would do is what most couple's do to each other: "Yeah—right, *prove it*!" "You're just crazy; there's no CIA tracking your thoughts—and you're definitely *not* Mary Magdalene's kid!" Think about what that would do. He would escalate to the extent of hitting me, breaking something or running out of the office. He would feel attacked and defensive; and that is exactly what couples typically do to each other. They remind me of a ping-pong tournament, back and forth with point and counterpoint, talking *at* each other, never being heard or feeling understood, until they end up flooding (Joe *loves* ping-pong).

'Active listening' is basically a psych 101 technique that, unfortunately, too many therapists never get beyond. There is a time and place for it however. You reflect back to the speaker what he is saying, in your own language:

Q: "So, what you are saying is that you are really hurting because you're constantly being harassed by the CIA?"

A: "Yea, Doc, and it's driving me *nuts*!"

Q:" Wow, that must be very upsetting for you."

A: "It sure is—and it seems like you are the only one I've spoken with so far who actually listens and understands me;" and he predictably becomes less agitated.

What people do not understand is that YOU DON'T HAVE TO AGREE TO BE A GOOD LISTENER. By temporarily putting your own agenda on the shelf, and *listening* to the other person first, whether you agree with them or not, you will inevitably find that they begin to calm down because they feel increasingly understood. I could be thinking 'CALL 911!'…but that does not mean I can't listen well. This definitely takes some discipline and self-control. Change what might not come naturally, however, and you may experience a surprising outcome.

RULE EIGHT: *Don't go to bed angry.*

When Reader's Digest surveys all those folks who have been married since the Pope was an altar boy, and asks them the secrets to the longevity of their marriage, they all seem to inevitably list this concept. This doesn't just address going to bed angry; it speaks to the idea of not holding grudges as well. Grudges in relationships are like cancer—a slow and certain death ensues; that being said, my buddies in A.A. talk about the 'H.A.L.T.' principle. They claim that a recovering alcoholic should never get "too Hungry, too Angry, too Lonely, or too Tired" because it renders them more vulnerable to acting out impulsively. Let's face it, sometimes it gets to be late at night; you're fuming at one another for some reason; you are both exhausted (H. *Angry.* L. *Tired*) and the potential is ripe for inviting Joe into your bedroom—not a pretty sight. What do you do? Before I give you the formula I must first present what I believe to be a workable definition of love. If Joe had his way, everyone would define love only by referencing emotions; thus the concepts of 'love at first sight;' 'loving you but not being *in* love with you;' 'falling in and out of love,' etc. Since 1978 I have worked in the field of human relations; I've seen it all, and as far as I can tell, 'Love' comes down to this:

*'You love a person to the extent to which you act in the loved-one's best interest, to the best of your ability, **regardless of how it feels.**'*

Those of you who are parents probably know exactly what this definition is all about. Many times I had to discipline my kids, even if my guts were wrenching, as they would cry, "I don't *like* you!" "It's nice to be liked," I would say, "but that's not in my job description—so get up to your room!" I acted in their best interest—*regardless of how it feels.* Please do not misinterpret this definition to imply that loving someone means doing what they want or what they *like;* it sometimes comes down to making very unpopular choices that nobody *likes,* but that have to be done in the loved-one's best interest.

With this understanding in mind, as well as the H.A.L.T. principle, imagine that it is very late at night; you are both exhausted, but there is considerable anger and tension between you that probably will not be settled that evening. Realistically, there is no way to eliminate the angry emotions before you go to bed, so, what do you do? *Regardless of how you feel,* a) Assure the person that you love him or her; b) go to bed, and c) continue tomorrow if necessary. In many cases, the supposed problem doesn't seem quite so urgent the next day; but if it still needs to be addressed, you can probably allow the CEO to tackle it rather than 'you know who.'

The amount of arguments people get into has little to do with how healthy or satisfying their relationships are; the *way* they argue, however, has everything to do with it. Write down the eight rules, post them in a place where you can review them on a regular basis, and gradually start to assimilate them into your style of relating to others—they're very 'cost-effective.'

7

How A Family Is Supposed To Work

We are living in increasingly desperate times, and the structure and functioning of our families are, arguably, the most important considerations relevant to healthy mental development and survival as a people. Despite the fact that it is a waste of time to blame our parents for *our* actions (although I have a few things to say about the media) our family life constitutes one of our most profound shaping influences. Of course the eight rules of good arguing, as I mentioned, can readily be applied to families; there are other relevant truths, however, that will come in pretty handy when interacting with family members whom you influence. What I am about to present may seem like a 'no brainer' to some, but to others it may serve as a saving guide through the insanity.

Get honest for a moment. Look back on a significant accomplishment or possession in your life. Now write down the work, sacrifice or pain it took; reflect on this...Without work, sacrifice or pain, you wouldn't value these things; why would this be any different for others?

Whether you are in the midst of raising a family of your own, or working in a setting that duplicates the family process, it always pays to at least have a healthy understanding of how it ought to be.

Returning to our analogy of the CEO and Joe the Custodian, it may not come as a surprise to discover that a family also runs much like a business. First let me present my opinion that I do not view 'democratic' families as very effective, for the most part. The analogy between a commune and a capitalistic business may apply here. "When you are paying the mortgage," I would tell my kids," then you'll have a whole lot more say, but until then the buck stops here." In a working business, there is always a hierarchy—a pecking order. The CEO and possibly the President should always present as a *unified front* (with disagreements worked out behind 'boardroom doors'). Of course parents may have different 'styles', usually comprising a "Rambo" and a "Florence Nightingale," but that does not mean they can't present as unified. I actually think that the perfect parent is a blend of someone who doesn't take any nonsense—but who also loves them to death. I have seen 'demon children' created by what I call the "Toxic Dyad" of two parents undercutting one another in front of the kids. Can you imagine the CEO and President arguing and sabotaging one another's decisions in front of the employees? The company would be split and chaos would ensue. The classic family therapy concept of 'triangulation' occurs when a child is allowed to 'divide and conquer'—what a mess. 'Employee input' is fine, and even essential in running a productive business, but executives should never lose their bearings. When employees have some say, they tend to "own" the new policies and contracts as opposed to simply putting up with the latest rendition of whatever the bosses decide. Getting input from the kids is great, but do not ever forget where the buck stops. The concept of the 'benevolent dictator' may fit. I have always agreed that "God loves them just as much" and that everyone has equal worth in the home and in the business; they should never, however, have *equal say.* If Joe and his peers had equal say as the executives, there would be anarchy, and bankruptcy.

On a slightly different note, if your kids ever decided to take you to court for being a bad parent (which I'm sure has been done) do you know what your legal 'job description' is? The wording may be slightly different in various states, but, basically it follows along the lines of this: You are legally responsible for providing food, clothing, shelter and 'reasonable supervision'—everything else comes up as "perks." Our country is raising a generation of children who know their 'rights' very well—but many have no clue or understanding about their 'wrongs.' Add this to the 'fast food' mentality of instant gratification: "I want what I want when I want it—and I want it NOW!" Many parents are either duped by the latest 'pop-parenting' ideas or they are trying to somehow make up for the way *they* were treated by their parents. The worst thing to do is to give everything to your kids that *you* never had, thus raising a generation of entitled, spoiled brats who expect the world owes them. Again and again, I appeal to *common sense* in your approach to life. Do you really appreciate anything that you didn't have to work or sacrifice for?—of course not. The formula always applies: *Pain* (in this case it comes in the form of sacrifice) + *Desire* + *Ability* = *Change*. I am convinced that, if you grow accustomed to some pain or sacrifice early in life, you will have an easier time assimilating the process as you grow; I think that is called 'character'. You can condition your mind through discipline, just like your body, to become ever stronger. Think about how 'cost-effective' it would be to instill this in your children as soon as possible. Before going out to do something fun, how about quickly straightening up the house or putting out the garbage? It will become 'second nature' to them to work prior to having fun or gaining some reward, rather than expecting something for nothing. I recall the hours I spent as a youth working out in the pool (I was a competitive swimmer) while so many of my friends were out partying or hanging out. I had plenty of 'fun' time, but it was a real sacrifice some days. As time progressed I honed my athletic skills, grew stronger and, eventually, I achieved national recognition in swimming, and I was offered full scholarships to several universities. The Marines have a bunch of slogans targeting competition and physical conditioning; one of the best one's I have heard is: "Pain is just weakness leaving the body." Whether physical, emotional or mental, truth is truth, and the formula is universal. Instant gratification and entitlement are character killers. Parents who engender these qualities in their children are either ignorant or selfish (it is more important for them to be 'liked' than to do what is in the kid's best interest). What a difference from the parent who sees every activity as an opportunity to teach their child qualities that build character, make them accustomed to sacrificing, enduring discomfort at times, and preparing them to develop a mind-set that serves them well for the rest of their lives.

Whenever you begin a new job, there is a process for all new employees called "orientation" in which you are educated about the benefits and consequences relevant to job performance—or lack thereof. Both the rewards and consequences are *predictable* and *consistent,* so there are no surprises. *That* places the outcome squarely in the hands of the employee (accountability). There is supposed to be equal and fair treatment for all new employees. Imagine how upset you would be if, out of nowhere, your supervisor just 'drops' some obscure rule on you that ends up docking you pay. In a family and in a business, predictable consequences are far more enforceable. Employees are better able to take responsibility for their actions abiding by the adage, "to be forewarned is to be forearmed." Dealing with kids is no different—it reflects the real world and prepares them to succeed. In understanding and bringing about change in your own mind or in the minds you influence, one must always apply the principle of reality, asking, "Does this reflect the 'real world'?" In the real world, and the business world, choices inevitably lead to consequences. One of the most ridiculous ideas about parenting I have ever heard, probably developed by 'experts' who have screwed up kids themselves, is the concept of never hinting that a child is"bad." I have often heard advice that you should discipline them *only* on the basis of their *behavior.* "It's not *you* that I'm upset with, Johnny, it's your *behavior."* Do you realize for one moment how bizarre this concept is? Heaven forbid we should even hint that Johnny is being bad—he'll develop a complex or something! Who the heck *did* the behavior? Can you imagine being pulled over by a police officer for speeding; the cop asks for your license and registration. "Sir," he says, "Don't be upset, I'm not giving *you* a ticket for speeding—I'm giving your *behavior* a ticket. Have a nice day."

> *RULE ONE: Unless it's life-threatening, **never** protect*
> *them from the consequences of their behavior!*

This leads to the first of two simple yet effective rules of parenting that reflect the formula for change on an interactive level:

Remember that *Pain* is the first part of the formula for real change. Providing the skills, hopefully through example, you can supply kids with the third essential component of the formula, and desire will hopefully develop along the way. Recall that the definition of love involves doing what is in the loved-one's best interest regardless of how it feels, and pain is necessary for change to occur—it is common sense. It is not about what you or they happen to like. Many times the situation calls for a somewhat 'robotic' response, not unlike when we train a dog. You certainly do not want to scream and yell at a dog in training; it's all about rewards, punishment, and outcome. Whether you are bringing about change in your own life, or in the lives of your loved-one's, you always keep on track when you adhere to the common sense formula for change—it is what works. Of course, because of your legal job description, it is your obligation to intervene if there ever comes a time when your child's safety may be jeopardized. If my little girl decided to stroll across route 84, I wouldn't say to my wife, "Let her go, honey, if she gets hit by an 18-wheeler, then she'll learn." Obviously, if her life is at risk, I really do not care what she has to say—she's out of there! With anything short of that, however, as much as it grieves me, I will compassionately allow her to suffer the consequences of her actions.

> *RULE TWO: Always follow through!*

The second rule of effective parenting is so simple, it is hard to understand how so many parents do not get it. I suppose, again, when Joe the Custodian is allowed to take over, common sense goes right out of the window. If most people in our society only adhered to the first rule and this rule, I am convinced that we would soon be back on point. The second rule is another incredibly simple one:

Whether you are a cop, a supervisor, a parent, or just working on yourself, following through provides a foundation for getting results. It also makes you *stop and think* before you make a decision. As a police officer, it would be a big problem to tell a perpetrator," look, if you do/don't do (fill in the blank) you will be arrested." The guy does/doesn't do it, and the officer says, again, "...now I really mean it—I'll give you one more chance;" and the guy does/doesn't do it again as you plead with him," listen, I'm not kidding around, I really mean it this time..." What a joke! As a parent, I have to think before I tell my kids what is going to happen, because, no matter what—I will always follow through. So if I let Joe take over and yell, in a moment of flooding, "I'm gonna *kill* you guys!" ...now I have to hide the bodies, worry about the DNA evidence, etc., it's too much of a hassle (just kidding). Think before you say it! My poor Dad would, unfortunately, often blurt out "No", prematurely, when my brother or I asked about doing something. At that point the game of wearing him out begins. "Dad, *pleeease* let us (fill in the blank); everybody else's Dad (that's everybody else's Mother's spouse) lets them;" 'No!" he would say again, and we would counter with endless pleading and rationalizations relevant to him being "unreasonable"... "Come on, Dad, just this one time...come on, *pleeease* ..." Eventually we would wear him out and he would inevitably cave in with, "OK!" What he didn't realize was that he unwittingly trained us to never give in, never give up, and nag him until he succumbed to our relentless onslaught. Parents just don't seem to understand that, by not following through, they are creating a powerful training program for their children. As someone who spent his entire life studying human behavior, I could not create a more effective regimen that would teach kids to 'endure and raise the stakes—never give up—never give in; and *keep* raising the stakes until you get what you want.'

Knowing that you have to follow through forces you to think about what you are going to say *before* you say it. That slow, deep breath before you react, standing by what you decide is in their best interest, eliminates the nagging and the endless arguing that so many parents describe. I would rather eat broken glass and crawl on the asphalt, on my knees for miles, rather than reverse my decision (you get the picture), and that forces me to think before I come up with a consequence or a decision with my kids—and it works. Of course it almost goes without saying that, as a parent, you need to 'practice what you preach' to the best of your ability. It never ceases to amaze me how someone smoking a cigarette and holding a scotch in his hand can exclaim, "If I ever catch you smokin' or drinkin'—I'll beat the #$%^&**## outta' you!" 'Do as I say, not as I do' doesn't work. That being said, the two simple rules of parenting, used effectively, would eliminate the sense of entitlement we encounter today with our youth. It would also go a long way in helping them to start early in forming a strong basis for following through with themselves. We all tend to eventually internalize what we are taught, whether we like it or not. It is much more cost effective to start as soon as possible in training our minds for success. If our parents didn't do it with us, we can do it for ourselves; it just takes a little more effort (desire). If we still have a chance to help form our kids, however, it is perhaps the most valuable gift we can give them. Although they may not appreciate it at the time, it will keep on giving long after the I-Pod or the X-Box wear out.

When you apply the two basic rules of parenting, you will implement them more effectively by also adhering to the pyramid concept. I learned about this model relevant to the use of force, while in the police academy. The pyramid represents the ever increasing levels of force needed to "control the action" of a perpetrator, and it makes perfect sense. It is predictable, reasonable, and it works. The higher up the pyramid you go, the more extreme is the force used; and it is the 'perpetrator' who ultimately decides just how high it goes. The officer applies force that is *only one step above* that used by the bad guy. If I ask a fellow to show his license and registration, which he is required to do by law, he has to present it, and it ends there. If, on the other hand, I ask for license and registration, and he exclaims, "F_ You Pig!" (Which has actually been said to me), we will go to the next level.

I would ask him to exit the vehicle, he gets searched, and his license is taken…if it stops there. If the driver wants to get in a fistfight with me, he is going to get maced or tazed (one step above on the pyramid). Should the driver decide to pull a knife on me, he will be coming to a gun fight with a knife—not a very smart idea. Of course the top of the pyramid is deadly force, which can happen in a split second; but it rarely goes there as long as the perpetrator realizes he doesn't have a chance of winning the fight. The kids, now grown, who were taught that the rules apply to everyone else but them, are the ones who 'don't get it'; these are the ones whose parents did not follow through in a predictable, reasonable and consistent manner. Being one step above them ultimately serves as prevention from further escalation of force. If, on the other hand, I meet him on the *same level*, perhaps finding a knife of my own when he pulls one out, he might believe he has a chance to win; and that could spell disaster. Unfortunately too many adult children were never taught by their folks that choices do lead to consequences. Coming across an adult child whose parents never followed through in a consistent and reasonable way can lead him to take a simple traffic stop and escalate it to a felony. In the public school system, so many teachers these days deal with the same phenomena as they bemoan the position of being given ever more responsibility, and less authority. The result of having so many kids out there who not only do not respect authority, but have parents who are eager to hire lawyers to threaten anyone who would dare to actually have them feel the consequences of their actions, has done much to further the decay of our society; these are the ones who will place the burden on police and other authority figures to do the job Mom and Dad neglected to do. Too many parents have relegated their children, who are rapidly becoming adults, to a distorted view of morality. It is no longer a point of 'right or wrong,' but, rather, who has the best attorney.

PAIN, the first part of the formula for change, can constructively be introduced via the two rules; and understanding the pyramid concept can guide you in a practical and predictable manner when implementing the rules. This reflects the *real* world and common sense; why would you not make it a foundation in the home?

"Deadly Force"

The officer is always only *one* step above, and it is the *perpetrator* who decides how high it goes.

(The higher up you go, the more extreme the use of force)

Just imagine pulling some guy over and asking him for his license and registration; he says,"F-You Pig!" and I pull out my asp (a collapsible 'Billy Club') and smash his skull! That is what is called 'excessive force'. This seems pretty obvious when discussing police work, but how many parents base their interventions on how *mad* they are? They don't say anything, or they speak too quickly, but when they are mad enough (that's when Joe takes charge) they blow up and yell, "THAT'S IT— YOU'RE GROUNDED FOR A MONTH!" (Parental 'excessive force'). They never follow through because the consequence is excessive, not thought out and logical, and they inevitably renege only to repeat the cycle again. 'Consistent, predictable' and 'reasonable' go right out the window and they slide right back into the infamous cycle of 'doing the same things, over and over again, expecting different results.' The two rules can only work when Joe stays in the basement!

A discussion about developing healthy young minds would fall short without briefly addressing the idea of chores. Chores should be introduced as soon as possible in a kid's life; prolonged gratification, discipline, responsibility and productivity (which we will talk about later) are all introduced by way of them. Make them fun. Charts with smiley faces, stars, etc. can serve as secondary rewards for kids who may find it difficult to delay gratification at first. Break down an age-appropriate list to be reviewed daily. The reward(s) are given at the end of the week. A 'perfect' week would involve a bonus of some kind. A week of too many daily prompts would result in penalties. 'Rewards,' however, must be constructed based on the Premack Principle[5]. Dr.Premack (who actually studied apes—go figure) found that, theoretically, what an 'organism' does in their spare time (naturally high frequency) is intrinsically rewarding to them. When parents are trying to figure out just what motivates a child, they sometimes come up blank. For some kids, being sent to their room is the *worst* thing that could happen to them; for some it is the best thing. Ultimately, whatever serves to increase a behavior is intrinsically reinforcing-no matter what you may think would be reinforcing to *you*. I suggest that parents simply watch what their kid does in his/her spare time and they will discover what works for motivation (desire); thus, establishing one of the steps in the formula. Never 'loan' children rewards ahead of time—it doesn't work.

One last comment about rewards is in order. Once you promise a child a reward that is contingent on a certain behavior, such as going to the movies for raking the lawn, *never* renege on it (That's the positive aspect of always following through). Can you imagine being told by your supervisor at work that, if you put in some extra time this week and produce X-amount of widgets, you will receive a hefty bonus? You put in the time, produce the widgets, but you get in an argument with your boss at the last minute, and he says, "That's it—now you're not getting that bonus I promised you." How many parents promise a certain reward for certain behaviors, which the kid does, only to take it away if he/she gets in a fight with his/her brother? Always follow through; find some other way to punish if you have to, but let him/her receive what he/she worked for. Just remember that the family goes a long way in influencing children, who eventually become the adults who will govern our country and, in turn, influence our society; change can be accomplished on the micro *and* macro level if we 'work smart.'

Just take a moment now to imagine the changes that would be brought about if you simply abided by the two basic rules here. Your family would undergo a very real 'revolution' for the better, even though it may not *feel* so good in the beginning. Now imagine what our society would be like if we, as a people, were to actually *follow through* in a reasonable and predictable manner when the law was broken. Politicians and criminals (is that redundant?) would have to be accountable for their actions, and make amends instead of hiring a high-priced lawyer to skirt around the consequences of their actions. People would actually have to sacrifice for their rewards in life, as opposed to suing for every little thing, or expecting the world to owe them a living. Why does this all sound so much like *common sense?* Because it *is!*

A family runs like a business, and the eight rules of good arguing can easily be applied here as well; abiding by the two essential rules of *good parenting*, however, could solve 90% of the problems in families, and ultimately in our society. Try to memorize the definition of love, from the previous chapter, and see if you can begin to integrate it with the two rules of parenting as you interact with family members—*regardless of how it feels.*

8

Unleashing The Power
Of Your Imagination

L et's return for a moment to the formula for change: *PAIN + DESIRE + ABILITY = CHANGE.* Pain, or discomfort, can be brought about in many ways. You can take advantage of the 'natural' pain that life brings you, such as physical discomfort, upsetting circumstances or emotional discord with others; or you can experience pain in the form of contrived situations such as when an intervention is performed. Most of our pain, however, is the direct or indirect result of poor choices, from drinking too much to impulsive actions that could end up in jail time, and it serves as a 'heads up' from God—if we listen and harness the energy thus produced.

My developmental psychology professor used to wisely remind us that "organization

> **Get honest** *for a moment. Have you ever caught yourself daydreaming or imagining the 'worst possible scenario' of something? If you could, just think about how it affected any desire to change. Did it motivate you or make you discouraged? Now take a moment to reflect on an accomplishment in your past. Can you recall ever experiencing a rush of anticipation right before it happened? Are you able to re-experience that rush by re-imagining the victory?*

inhibits reorganization," meaning that, like a flow chart or a decision tree, our choices and ensuing actions may close some doors in our future as well as open others. Regardless of whether the pain we have experienced was brought about needlessly through our own poor decisions, or whether it came to us by way of natural circumstances in which we had little choice—ALL PAIN IS GOOD PAIN if we allow it to become part of our formula for change. Understanding the way your mind works (e.g., A-B-Cs), and training it to implement the changes you desire by developing necessary skills, become the 'meat' of this book. You are long overdue to knock off the *Wouldas-Couldas*-and-*Shouldas* of past mistakes, stop paying the toll, and use the formula to launch yourself out of the 'Poor-me s.' Once pain or discomfort is introduced into your life, along with some desire, the arena for real change then proceeds to *ability* (skills). It is in the realm of our beliefs, as we have seen, that much of the battle is fought; and skills, or lack thereof, become the deciding factor. We have already presented some cognitive skills for identifying and replacing irrational self-talk (mostly geared at keeping Joe in the basement). It is now time to explore and utilize the tremendous power of the imagination, which is a skill heretofore not even 'imagined' (pardon the play on words).

Let me pose a question to you: What is more powerful, the imagination or the will? Every year around graduation time, I perform various hypnosis stage shows for local High Schools. It is amazing how these young adults cannot straighten out limbs that are 'stiff and rigid,' as they awkwardly attempt to hop around the stage. The Valedictorian can't count to ten—no matter how hard he/she tries. I usually pick out the most macho tough guy, and make him give birth to a baby (at least that's what he believes). The part of the show that usually dispels the skeptics' disbelief in 'whether they're *really* hypnotized' is when I make myself invisible to the participants. They cluster together around an invisible 'Ghost Busters' gun, absolutely terrified, in an effort to control the hideous invisible ghoul causing the microphone to somehow float mysteriously in space without any form of support. Despite any debates regarding the nature of hypnosis, the fact remains that the imagination, when properly harnessed, can form the basis of the most amazing feats. While on stage, I can easily select the strongest volunteer to attempt to pick up a 50 dollar bill while his/her feet are 'glued to the floor' (in their imagination), and, no matter how hard they try, that bill simply cannot be grasped.

Imagine that there is a 200 foot long, 4-by-12 metal beam placed approximately one foot off the ground. Let's add some fairly powerful fans, placed at intervals along the way, blowing gusty wind as you walk or crawl along the beam. Your mission, 'should you decide to accept it' (it's that T.V. influence again), is to make it to the end of the beam without falling off; sound hard? What if I upped the stakes and told you that successfully making it across the length of the beam would result in a $10,000 reward? Most people would not have any problem at all making it across the beam. Despite the *same level of difficulty* how many of you would take on the same challenge if that same beam was supported between the former Twin Towers? The imagination *is* stronger than the will!

The mind is, in some ways, unfathomable. At the beginning of this book I had mentioned only a few striking facts about its power to create our 'reality.' Consider the fact that our imagination can transcend space and time; that is why we get upset about something that might have happened *years* ago. By merely thinking about an event, your mind 'fools' your body into believing that the event is actually happening *now*. What else would explain the emotional and physical reaction you get simply by recalling a distressing event from the past? People describe literally *re-experiencing* past events when they recall them. When an event from the past was perceived as particularly emotionally charged (Joe was clearly at the helm), it can be recalled quite vividly; this is called a 'Flashbulb memory'. Flashbulb memories and images, however, may not necessarily be accurate. Emotional overtures, preconceived notions, modifying the events throughout time ('Re-scripting'), misinformation, context, cognitive distortions, can all play with memories and their resulting images in your mind; thus creating what you would refer to as your 'reality.' Just as the mind can 'distort' images, depending on the aforementioned factors, it can also 'modify' them to work for you dynamically. Applying what you are learning about the formula for change, having an idea of what is healthy, influencing others close to you, disputing and replacing cognitive distortions, harnessing your addictive potential and re-creating your reality through your imagination, can add up to a life-changing process that will turn things around in a powerful way. Imagine really tapping into this resource!

Awhile ago we were sitting around recalling memories from years gone by. My oldest son, Nathanael, came out with a statement that nearly floored me. He said, "Hey Dad, remember the time when you beat the crap out of me?" "What are you talking about," I replied, "I never beat the crap out of you." "Sure you did," he came back, and proceeded to tell of an incident that allegedly occurred when he was about 11 or 12 years old. I had come home from a long, arduous day at work, tired and short on patience. Ben and Nathanael were fighting, as siblings do, and Nate decided to give Ben a thump on the back. Ben, true to form, let out a blood-curdling shriek that sounded like a tyrannosaurus rex in labor. I yelled, "Knock it off—or I'll give you something to really be upset about!" A moment later, Nate wacked Ben again, who predictably over dramatized the incident with a grimaced look, writhing movements indicative of a cardiac arrest and ,of course, the accompanying 'death gurgle'—that was *it*!

Nathanael saw the homicidal look in my eyes and the characteristic bulging vein in my neck that gave the undeniable message that now, 'HEADS WERE GONNA ROLL!' He immediately lurched for the steps and ran upstairs helter-skelter for the sanctuary of our bedroom, which had the only door in the house that *might* withstand my forced entry. I bounded up the stairs right behind him, caught him by the back of his collar, and literally picked him off his feet while his legs were still running. In a fit of anger, I dropped him onto the floor. Gesturing with clenched fist, I slowly belabored each word as I exclaimed, "IF-YOU-HIT-YOUR-BROTHER-ONE-MORE-TIME-I'M-GOING-TO-HIT-YOU! DO YOU UNDERSTAND ME?!" (Of course I broke the 'no rhetorical questions' rule, as well as the parenting rule about following through). Nevertheless, Nathanael was not used to seeing me lose it like that, and in his young mind he created a 'Flashbulb memory' that was re-scripted, with time, to have him believe I actually did beat the crap out of him. I was glad that Ben was a witness to the event, and he validated my retelling of it.

Whether something happened or not, our images eventually become part of our reality-even if they sometimes don't make sense or cannot be articulated. As children, we all have a storehouse of pre-verbal images, filtered through our young perceptions that play a powerful role in every aspect of our reality today. Is it any wonder that 'False Memory Syndrome' became a primary focus of Forensic Psychology some years ago? Fortunately, as images and memories were created, they can be *modified* to become part of our formula for change.

In order to fully utilize the power of imagery in bringing about changes, you must first become adept at progressive muscle relaxation (PMR). PMR, fortified by guided imagery, can create a conduit for your mind to absorb life-changing suggestions very effectively; it becomes a modality that can short-cut the 'percolation' effect I described in chapter two. Here is an example of a passive PMR exercise that you can practice ('active' PMR involves the alternate tensing and relaxation of each muscle group):

Begin by finding a comfortable, safe location where no one will bother you. Reading this exercise onto a recording device ahead of time may be more effective for you as you can then simply listen to your own recorded voice played back while you relax. Some people like complete silence while others enjoy mellow music or natural sounds such as ocean waves or rainfall in the background; I prefer some steady noise, such as a fan or humming air conditioner. When you record, allow your voice to be slow and monotone; soothing and hypnotic-like. You will notice that there are many pauses during the script; take your time and count slowly in your head to 5 or 10 before you proceed after each pause; remember, slower is usually better. Using a set of headphones to listen to this script being played back to you can better eliminate distractions.

Lie down and uncross your arms and legs. Loosen any tight fitting clothing and place a pillow under your knees and behind your head if you like. Take a slow, deep breath, in through your nose and slowly out through your mouth while pursing your lips for added control on the exhale; breathe down low from your stomach. Try not to let your chest rise and fall as you breathe; instead, imagine a balloon right under your navel and allow your belly to rise and fall with each breath. If you ever watch puppy dogs or babies breathe when they are sleeping, you will see them belly-breathing. 6 Now roll your eyes high up toward the top of your head, and with your eyes still rolled up, slowly close your eyelids (pause). You might experience some rapid fluttering in your eyes, which is one of the signs people show when they are allowing themselves to really let go (pause); the fluttering will gradually go away as you go deeper and deeper relaxed (pause). Imagine now that you are floating, floating...perhaps softly floating downward like a feather being softly caressed by the warm breeze (pause); or are you floating upward, gently, like a balloon (pause)?...or, maybe you can imagine yourself like a leaf, floating comfortably on the surface of a still pond (pause). Notice now that as you imagine yourself floating, you are feeling more and more relaxed with each and every breath (pause).

Imagine now the muscles all around the top of your head are becoming like loose, heavy rubber-like...just letting go, and the top of your head is becoming heavy and relaxed (pause). Ever so gently, now, imagine a wave of heavy relaxation slowly moving down around your forehead (pause), your ears and toward the back of your neck (pause), and then slowly, the warm wave of heavy relaxation begins to move into your eyes, the muscles around your eyes, your eyelids and cheeks (pause). The heavy wave begins to gently work its way down into your jaw (pause) and even your tongue is feeling heavy (pause) as your tongue and jaw hang loose, separating your teeth ever so slightly. The wave of heavy, soothing relaxation is now moving down your neck and into your shoulders (pause), so that you are becoming aware of the weight of your head. Gently and slowly the wave begins to roll down your chest and upper back, soothing and relaxing the muscles as it goes (pause). Feel the heaviness now as the relaxation moves down into your upper arms (pause), and down slowly into your lower arms (pause), your wrists (pause), and slowly down your hands to the very tips of each finger (pause). Now, breath in slowly in through your nose, and then more slowly out through your mouth as the wave of relaxation begins to move its way down your lower back (pause) and down through your stomach as it soothes and relaxes all the organs within the torso (pause). The heavy, loose, relaxing wave begins to travel down through your hips and buttocks (pause), feeling the heaviness of your body...heavy and limp (pause); down through the pelvic area, heavy, heavy...and down into your thighs (pause). The wave of warm, heavy relaxation begins now to drift down around your knees, and into your calves and shins (pause); it moves down, now, into your feet, and slowly down to the tips of each of your toes (pause). Now feel that body, heavy...so heavy; limp, heavy and relaxed (pause). Slowly and gently breathe in through your nose... hold it for a moment (pause)...then slowly let the air escape through your mouth, feeling relaxed, heavy and perfectly at peace.

Most relaxation-type exercises follow a similar script focusing on progressive muscle relaxation (PMR) and abdominal breathing such as this. You can customize whatever works best for you, but once you record your relaxation exercise, it is time to compose a script that paves the way for powerful changes in your mind. Remember that your mind has virtually no boundaries; what I mean is that you can go beyond space, time and even 'logic'...if that's what works for you. Go beyond 'natural laws' with your imagination—it's what creativity is all about. This is 'The Bomb!'... (Way better than TV).

Composing a script for change: Target whatever it is in your life that you want to address, and have a firm idea of where you want to go with it. You can compose this by way of an imaginary movie that can be freeze-framed, blown up, cut and pasted; copied and arranged with whomever and/or whenever you decide[7]. Try to use all your senses; that is, introduce smell, touch, hearing, tasting and, of course, seeing wherever possible.

Right after you go through the PMR, you would then begin with something such as this (if, for example, you were targeting weight-loss):

(PMR)...Now imagine that you are standing at the top of a flight of ten steps, looking down to a very stylish waiting room. I'm going to count down from 10 to 1, you can count silently along with me; and with each count downward, you can take a step downward. With each step downward, you will feel yourself going deeper, and even deeper relaxed. When we reach the first step, all the way down, you will be in the comfortable, stylish waiting room; there will be no one in the room but you. "10"...begin to feel the heaviness in your arms and legs; down to "9"...heavy arms, heavy legs; deeper to "8"..as you feel the heavy relaxation flowing all through you; "7"... down deeper, and deeper; down to "6"...heavy, heavy, heavy; deeper now to "5"...as you feel it flow all through you; down now to "4"... and "3"... as the deeper you go, the more comfortable you become; down to "2"...way, way, down; and all the way down to "1". Now you are in the beautiful waiting room. Look slowly around, overlooking nothing. Notice the plush, leather couches, and the soft, comfortable lounge chairs; a deep, rich brown with glossy expensive wooden accents. You become intrigued with the intricate pattern of the wallpaper...fascinating; and then you detect a mild fragrance, perhaps it is lavender, as you look up to notice an ornate, full-length mirror in front of

you. As you gaze upon the mirror, you become entranced with the figure before you...a shapely, lean and well-kept body. It is you at the weight your are meant to be. Stare at this strong, healthy image before you which becomes ever clearer before your eyes. 8 Take your hands and slowly roll them down the sides of your body...feel how good it is to be at the weight you are meant to be...and notice how you are standing, firm, tall and confident. All of a sudden you notice the figure in the mirror has a box, and it is being given to you, through the glass...amazing. You take the box in your hands and find yourself overwhelmingly curious about what is inside. Unlatch the hinged top of the box and slowly open it. It appears dark inside as you look deeply within. Your mind seems entranced with the contents of this mysterious box...and then something emerges; it is what has kept you from achieving your weight goal. Does it make a sound? Examine it closely...what is it? (Pause) Study it, and...allow your powerful unconscious mind to gently let you know what you will do with what the box is letting you know...listen to what it is telling you...etc.

You could compose *anything* about any topic. Here's a simple example of one about public speaking: *Imagine that you are sitting in an old movie theatre. The damp smell of old curtains and velour seats is intermingled with stale popcorn. You are all alone, sinking down into the seat, anticipating the movie that is about to play. The thick crimson curtains on the stage begin to part slowly, revealing the screen behind them, as the house lights dim. You hear the projector clicking as the flashes of white on the screen herald the movie that is about to start. The screen comes alive with a bright white light, and the frames of what you are about to see seem to flicker faster until a scene appears before you; a scene of you walking toward what appears to be a stage. You watch yourself, fascinated, as you walk up to a podium, hundreds of people in the audience before you, anticipating what you are about to say. (At any time, you can freeze-frame, relax, and continue whenever you like) See yourself, feel yourself, confident and poised, ready to speak clearly and authoritatively about the subject you have chosen for this evening. Your notes are in front of you in case you would like to glance at them , but you are so well prepared that it is not necessary...it just flows from you as you entertain and enlighten the enthusiastic listeners. Before you know it, the speech is over, and the crowd applauds-what a rewarding experience! You take a slow, deep breath, thank your audience; you walk away filled with confidence and looking forward to the next opportunity to speak publically—you're feeling ON TOP OF THE WORLD!*

Obviously, the examples of guided imagery scripts are truly limitless; as limitless as the imagination itself. I will present just one more here, however, that was previously published in *Law Officer* Magazine as part of an article on Stress Inoculation Training for Police Officers: *Get comfortable, and close your eyes. Breathe in slowly through your nose and out slowly from your mouth. Begin to consciously relax the muscles in your body starting at the top of your head and gradually working down through your toes (PMR). In this relaxed state, it becomes easier to imagine things.*

Now, begin to imagine yourself at a traffic stop. It's a slightly overcast early evening with a cool breeze blowing, moderately heavy traffic, and the daylight is just about gone. See the registration, color and make of the car as you call it in. Feel the radio mic in your hand and even smell the inside of the car.

As the dispatch copies the transmission, notice that you're feeling uneasy for some reason. You put on your hat, grab your flashlight and exit your cruiser. As you reach over to click on your two-way, you slowly walk toward the driver's side of the stopped vehicle. Cars whiz by, and you feel the breeze on your face. You ask the driver to roll down his window and note movement in the rear seat. Suddenly your two-way interrupts with Dispatch reporting the vehicle as stolen.

Instantly, your heart starts to race, and two passengers exit and begin to run. Your attention is momentarily divided, but you focus on the more immediate threat-the driver's door flies open! You realize you're telling yourself, "Oh my God, I'm in danger!" But then, you freeze the scene, take a slow deep breath, and forcefully tell yourself to, "cover or conceal!" You identify the distress (fear) and vigorously reframe it into eustress (aggression). You draw your weapon and yell a command to the driver—you're in control, using the adrenaline rush to adapt and overcome.

The world was taken aback when the Russian Olympic weightlifters broke the power lifting record that was supposed to be unbeatable. How did they do it? They later admitted that they practiced exactly what I have just presented here. They first became proficient at PMR, then they composed detailed guided imagery scripts in which they 'saw' themselves repeatedly walking down to the weight bar, taking a deep breath, and jerking the massive weight up, over their shoulders for the record-breaking lift—and then they *did it!* What the mind can conceive, the body can achieve; and training your mind by using your imagination in this way, is the key to making it a reality in your life.

The imagination, by way of progressive muscle relaxation (PMR) and guided imagery exercises, can be utilized in amazing ways that unleash incredible power to bring about changes. Take a moment to practice PMR, maybe record a script that you like, and then compose a scenario that targets a specific change you want in your life. Practice it for 21 days, straight, and see what happens!

9

The Secret Of Happiness

"I only want to be happy—is that too much to ask?" How many times have you heard *that?* Typically, when I get this common plea, I respond with something along the line of this: I believe that happiness is a *byproduct* of correct thinking and living. If you pursue happiness only for the sake of happiness you may have a good chance of having it pass you by. On the other hand, happiness inevitably comes to you when you live life healthily and follow the guidelines that I'm presenting in this book. I have given you a simple formula for change; eight guidelines for arguing well, and two clear rules for influencing children under your care that could conceivably be one of the most easy solutions to bringing about needed changes in your life and the lives of your loved-ones. That being said, I will now give you what I think is the formula for happiness. Let me say, as an aside, that

Get honest for a moment. Have you ever felt truly happy even if it was for a brief moment? What was going on at that time? Now let me ask you, do you know anyone whom you would honestly think is happy? Reflect here...Jot down what you might attribute to their happiness—really. Do you think that the change(s) you desire in your life will make you happy? If so, how so? Now compare all this with what you will read in this chapter.

this topic has been on my mind since I was an adolescent; so I have researched it for over forty years, and I have narrowed it down to a brief acronym : P C P (...and I don't mean 'angel dust').

The first thing you need to be happy is a sense of *Purpose*. We are 'hard-wired' with a spiritual component that must be satisfied in some way. Theologians often comment that, within each of us, there is a 'God shaped hole.' Think about how many people live like animals, with very little thought about what life is really all about. They eat, defecate, sleep, reproduce...and die. They only live to acquire 'stuff' or to achieve certain goals—but to what end? Jesus once said, "What good is it for a man to gain the whole world, and yet lose or forfeit his very self?" (Luke 9:25). It reminds me of a variation of a popular saying, "He who dies with the most toys-*still dies.*" Can you imagine being on your death bed? If you could have your way, what would you want people or loved ones to be saying about you; what do you want to be remembered by? "Oh, yeah, he sure had a nice car;" or, "What a nice house she had." It sounds ludicrous when it is put that way but, think about it, what *is* your purpose for living? Think of how much more gratifying it would be to hear them saying something such as, "Wow, she certainly touched a lot of lives," or, "What a great Dad, and a terrific friend when I knew him, I couldn't help but see God's love shining through." Anyone can disagree with me about this but, as I often quote, "IT IS WHAT IT IS," whether you like it or not. This spiritual component within all of us *has* to be addressed, and satisfied, as part of the 'bigger picture' of what we live for, or it amounts to nothing, and we're left empty and unfulfilled. You can try to fill it with money, or sex, or relationships, or accomplishments, or *whatever*, but you are going to come up short unless you target a 'higher power' as part of the formula—feed that spirit!

The second component of the formula for happiness deals with our nature, again, relevant to those around us. We must have a sense of *Connectedness* to others whether we like it or not. I realize that this can be a blessing or a curse, but I am convinced that we are not meant to be alone. Of course, this can be a continuum, but we all desire on some level to be 'connected' to a group, a family, another person, a race, a culture, etc. Some folks seem fine feeling connected to only one or two others, while some seem to just be more gregarious. Having a sense of connectedness to a country or culture appears to meet this need in certain individuals, while many feel more 'worthy' and fulfilled being connected to a cause of some sort. No matter how you look at it, however, 'No man is an island.' Despite our moments of hurt, when we temporarily wish we could just run away and live on a desert island, all alone, we inevitably come face-to-face with our true nature; one in which we need to perceive ourselves as having connections. If I were to repeatedly ask you, "Who are you?" you would have to reference your connections, on some levels, in order to truly identify yourself; it is in your nature, as I said, and to deny it is to deny your very 'self.'

The final part of the formula for happiness comes to us in the form of *Productivity.* We are created to be productive on some level; it is also an integral part of our nature. Keep in mind, however, that a sense of productivity is based on very individual criterion—each person's perception (belief). I have seen some older people feel quite productive 'putsing' around the house, toying with their garden; others, on the other hand, come across as never believing they are doing quite enough despite working two jobs, raising a family, and pursuing their doctorate in their 'spare' time—usually the result of a profound sense of inadequacy. As with everything we experience, our perceptions (self talk) ultimately determine what *we* consider to be "Purpose," "Connectedness," or "Productivity."

There was a fascinating ABC special in April of 1996, hosted by John Stossel, addressing the subject of 'Happiness in America' (I suppose T.V. has some redeeming features). Three big-time lottery winners were interviewed. Despite the fact that just about everyone you speak with claims they would "love to win the lottery," the individuals interviewed were miserable. The process goes something like this: You win, say, a cool ten million dollars—whoopee! Naturally, you pay for all the meals, maybe the vacations, and even some loans that your good friends incur, because you have more than enough money 'to spare'. After awhile, others come to expect you to pick up the tab, and you start to get resentful. When you choose not to pay for something, you get 'attitude,' and maybe some jealousy from the folks you thought were your buddies. Next thing you know, you have 'relatives' coming out of the woodwork, and everybody has a hand out. You grow increasingly more distrustful, resentful and alienated from others. It doesn't take much time until you become trapped in a self-made prison, and, despite all that money, you find yourself depressed, lonely and wondering how it all got this way.

I guess money really *can't* buy happiness. It's amazing how the new millionaires interviewed were on anti-depressants, miserable, resentful, and a couple actually attempted suicide or seriously thought about it often. On the other hand, Stossel interviewed a paraplegic man who taught potential new citizens English as a second language. He was as happy as a pig in the mud, despite his seemingly tragic physical disability. He had *Purpose, Connectedness* or *Productivity*—go figure.

If my formula for happiness is accurate, than what I am about to say will come as no surprise. There was an informal survey conducted, as part of the same ABC documentary, in which various sub-groups in America were rated relevant to their overall sense of 'Happiness'. Guess who came out on top? The Amish. When you think about it, they are the most *Productive, Connected,* and *Purposeful* people in our country. They exemplify the three qualities as no other; it simply makes sense. They adhere to the Protestant work ethic completely; everything they do is referenced to their spiritual lives; and their sense of connectedness is all encompassing. Before you decide to dress 'plain' and trade in your Chevy for a buggy, however, remember that, despite individuality, the three principles, in balance, can be applied to anyone, anywhere. The three components of the formula, as I said, must work together in balance, or they become distorted.

There was an adage my theology professor used to say; "Any truth held in isolation brings perversion." To reiterate, anything that is pulled out of context tends to create a fuzzy mess. Magazines and politicians are notorious for pulling certain "truths" out of the context from which they were stated, thus distorting the original meaning. Whenever I receive one of those controversial e-mails touting some supposed "fact", my buddy Al has always clarified the bits of information by encouraging me to run it all through 'Snopes.com.' Perspective and balance inevitably become the 'touch stone' of truth—the 'Snopes' of reality. This concept particularly applies to the formula for happiness. Together the three ideas make perfect sense, but when applied separately, apart from the others, each concept becomes twisted and perverted. Let's consider this in a practical way: If I only have a sense of purpose, but lack connectedness and productivity, I become a religious recluse of sorts, good to nobody. With only a sense of connectedness, and no purpose or productivity, I am nothing more than a human lemming, following aimlessly anyone who directs me; all for the sole sake of being part of a group; this is the 'stuff' that cults are made of. Finally, Productivity without the others devolves into the most obvious perversion—*Workaholism!* Unfortunately, we tend to promote Workaholism in this country, thus producing a dead materialism, devoid of true purpose and meaning. This particularly insidious distortion of the formula not only leaves us empty and unfulfilled, it spreads its' poison to our children who, in turn, become our leaders.

As far back as 1988 a researcher by the name of John Conges wrote an article for the *American Psychologist* journal in which he correctly predicted the potential disaster that awaits us. Remember back in the 60's when youth were all about society and 'fellow man?' They decried and denounced the whole idea of 'filthy possessions.' Our wealthy, spiritually bankrupt culture has finally created the fruits of its ideology; a youth devoid of values that espouse any concern for others. Once spirituality and community consideration was ripped out of our system, and materialism was elevated to become our new 'God,' 'Generation X' morphed into a society that promotes the ego above all else. Wealthier and more miserable than ever, the 'Me Generation' (also called,' the Millennium' generation), with its sense of entitlement, has replaced the values of the 60's with a complete reversal of priorities.

The very last things our youth seem to be concerned with these days are society and the welfare of others. "Me First," has become the contemporary mantra—and *Productivity*, apart from true purpose and connectedness, has created this societal cancer. *Any truth held in isolation brings perversion!*

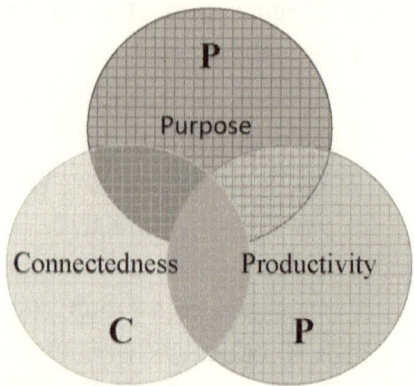

Whether you are considering the formula for change or happiness, the precept applies: they must be inclusive, with all three parts being kept in balance. In addition to the commonsense rules of good arguing, and parenting, these simple, yet profound practical truths and guidelines can potentially change the way you think and act. The final chapters will bring them all together so that you can apply them in your life.

Consider any time in your life when you felt 'out of touch' with yourself or others; what was missing—*purpose, connectedness* or *productivity?* Without all three working together, in balance, the formula for happiness does not apply, and the result is emptiness. Take a moment to review your life, and identify what part of the formula may be missing for you; is it worthy of change now?

10

Bringing It All Together

Imagine yourself in a very crowded elevator; so crowded that it's almost impossible to turn around. Someone behind you keeps bumping you, and poking you…and you are getting increasingly provoked. He keeps poking and poking, and you're getting more and more upset. What are you thinking? Most people would think that this guy's a rude ass who needs to be put in his place, right? 'Joe' just *loves* this kind of situation. You are determined to 'give him a piece of your mind' as soon as the elevator stops. When the doors finally open you step out and turn around to straighten this idiot out—and he's wearing dark glasses and sporting a cane—he's blind! Does that change what happened? No. Does it change how you *now* perceive it-what you *believe* about it? Yes. Our perceptions (beliefs) about past or present 'facts' *always*

> **Get honest** *for a moment. What do you really want to change in your life? As you have read thus far, are you able to imagine it happening for you; and are you now able to truly believe that the formula can work? Reflect…and write down what has realistically held you back from your change(s). Are you starting to appreciate pain, develop desire (which can involve HOPE); and are you getting an idea of working on your abilities within the context of happiness and love?*

create our 'reality.' Our reality defines our life, and profoundly affects our physical and emotional wellbeing. Interestingly, I posed the same elevator analogy to one of my clients, who just happened to be a rather tough Cop with a lot of anxiety. After setting the stage, I asked him what he would be thinking about the guy behind him in the elevator, poking him; he stated, "I would think the guy's an A-Hole!' When I introduced the part about getting out of the elevator and turning around to find out the guy is blind, I asked, "So what would you think then?" He exclaimed in a 'badda-bing' tone, "I'd think he was a *blind* A-Hole!" This analogy not only exemplifies the role our beliefs (self-talk) play in our reality, but it brings up a very relevant truth about looking at our past. Our beliefs, past, present or future, make all the difference in the world we *experience*. As I said in the beginning of this book, dwelling on the past, as so many therapists tend to do, is usually not cost-effective; an occasional look back, however, can yield some useful stuff that, when viewed from our present perspective, helps us to re-evaluate past events in the light of a different world—attaching different *meanings* to our history. This is powerful. The application of our formula for change, with the increasingly skillful use of the A-B-Cs, can not only help you look back on past events with a new perspective; it can enable you to re-create a reality that makes a difference in your current life. Using the techniques, understanding how your mind works, and incorporating the formula for change, can be applied to any past or *present* circumstances in your life to make an impact for you today. When you start to become proficient, and you assimilate this understanding with a working foundation of the formula for happiness, you will have successfully 'changed your mind.'

Let's lay it out and bring it all together for you now in a way that provides you with the common sense, hands on approach promised when you first picked up this book. The very first thing you need to ask yourself is: "What are my goals, and are they possible?" Writing things down not only forces you to use the higher centers of the brain; it makes you really **'Operationalize' whatever you are defining as a goal**. When someone says that they want "to never worry again about my children," I have no choice but to point out that they are being unrealistic. Worry less, and/or not *obsessing* is doable. When you operationalize something, you force yourself to articulate or write the desired change in a manner that is clearly understood and specific. "I want to exercise more, and quit smoking," would be an operational definition; better yet would be something along the line of, "I want to exercise at least five times a week, for 20-30 minutes a day." Whether you are trying to make a point with someone else, or attempting to bring about changes in your own life, *specific* is almost always better. One of the first things I tell potential clients is that "I'm like a mechanic." You wouldn't go to a mechanic with your car and simply tell him, "FIX IT." He would have to narrow down the presenting problem to specifics of *what exactly* you want fixed. "I want the noise in the rear end to stop," would be much more workable. When you write down, specifically, what you want to change, you will find that half the stuff you toy within your brain is unrealistic and undoable nonsense. Of course, the more desperate or emotional you become relevant to change, the more likely you are to allow 'Joe' to take the helm...and then bring on the late-night infomercials!

You know, you can lead that horse to water—*and you can make him very thirsty!* It is possible, as I pointed out earlier in this book, to 'raise your bottom,' as well as those of others. You can create your 'wish list' of changes, refine and eliminate what comes up as unrealistic, prepare yourself to 'sandbag' for the 'firefight' that will ensue; but the formula for change, with *all three components,* will always come into play. Is it going to be worth the *pain,* or discomfort that it will cost? Before any executive makes a major business decision, there must be a cost-benefit analysis—and Joe must not be in charge. How do you tell if the change is worth it, or even something that is worthy of consideration? When my son, Benjamin, went to Africa for a summer missions trip, he experienced a culture of people who were largely uneducated in a way we know. That is, there were superstitions that seemed to hurt them, such as when they place their children's faces over boiling water in order to purge the 'demons.' There were some tribes that believed if they had enough sex with a young girl, the men could eliminate AIDS. On the other hand, there were practices and beliefs, foreign to us, that indigenous people were privy to that enabled them to survive in a harsh environment. The question ultimately becomes,' what *is* progress?' This must be addressed prior to coming up with goals in your life.

Here, the question becomes more important than the 'solution.' *What do you want?* If the ultimate goal is *Happiness,* than we already are on our way to understanding and orchestrating something. Again, the more specific and operational goals are amenable to true change. Is the change goal *healthy?* Is your quality of life truly improved by the goal(s)? If so, then we can move on to the techniques and/or intervention(s) that will begin to bring it to fruition. I'm sure that, as you look back on your life, there are more than a few instances when you can now realize it was a good thing that your desires or prayers were *not* answered in a way you had originally hoped. Remember that girl who you just *had* to have, when you were a teenager? The old saying: "Be careful what you ask for-you might get it," is not too far off the mark is it? What this all comes down to is this: **Come up with goals that adhere to the definition of love**—for yourself or for others. Remember, *Love* is acting in the loved-one's best interest (whether that means yourself or others) regardless of how it feels. This is easy to understand when it comes to our dealing with kids or friends or spouses; but what about applying it to ourselves? Regardless of how it feels, just what *is* in your overall best interest? If we were to consider coming up with goals for some of the natives in Africa my son came across, we would have to question them about what exactly they would like as an *outcome.* Would they want to reduce or eliminate the AIDS epidemic amongst themselves, or perhaps enhance the longevity of their children? What I might consider as a worthy goal may just not be the same for you. Be pragmatic when coming up with your goals; is the outcome going to be something you really want? If I come up with a goal to make a million dollars within the next five years, does that truly reflect something that is in my best interest, or am I inviting

'Joe' to steer me? Remind yourself that *feelings* are not only the slaves of the past, they are the source of immaturity, needless pain, and rash decision-making that ultimately could hurt you and others—if they're not kept in their place.

The goal(s) you come up with must always consider the formula for happiness. When you create a goal for change, does it fit nicely into the balance of *all three* aspects of the secret of happiness? For example, would an operational goal of exercising five hours a day, seven days a week, fit the balance of *Purpose, Connectedness* and *Productivity* in your life? You will find that many goals automatically eliminate themselves as you apply the formula for happiness in their construction. There are certainly moments when various aspects of your life, relevant to the formula for happiness, become emphasized. If you are unemployed, for example, it goes without saying that more of an emphasis has to be placed on *Productivity* for awhile. Nobody is always in perfect balance all the time; keeping your eye on the prize, however, will guide you and give perspective even in the midst of turmoil. Keeping an eye on the formula for happiness, as it applies to you, can serve as a psychological 'surge protector' when developing your goal(s) for change.

Prior to creating any goal(s) for change, and implementing the changes, it is wise to take a little time to develop a working 'diagnostic' of your current functioning. This is just a fancy way of telling you that it is cost-effective for you to **create a current functioning baseline** to determine how 'off' you may be these days. Read through the A-B-Cs, and try to write down, or at least acknowledge the extent and type of cognitive distortions you are buying into these days. How are you doing relevant to your use of *Dichotomous Thinking, Emotional Reasoning, Filtering* or *Catastrophizing*? Before you can begin introducing changes, you must first assess where you are at *now*, and please don't give me the *Shoulds*; begin where you are, not where you 'should' be. If I were going to call you to ask for directions somewhere, it would be foolish and impractical to attempt anything until you knew my present location. Directions to Albany would be quite different for someone coming from Georgia than they would be for someone stuck in Seattle. Your functioning *now* becomes the starting point of intervention. Your physical and emotional resources, talents, abilities and circumstances all need to be taken into consideration at this time, but don't sell yourself short. Back in my days as a competitive swimmer, my coach always emphasized that I must compete against myself; swim against the clock, and push for my best time, no matter what the other swimmers were doing. The moment I 'swam against the other swimmers' I ended up 'swimming their race,' and my times were slower. You will learn from the past, keep an eye on the future, but you *live* in the present; live in *your* present, and this is where all the change occurs. Run your own race, but push the envelope!

Once you develop a working goal, specifically designed with your current functioning and the formula for happiness in mind, you are ready to apply a practical way of 'stepping up to the plate'. Many years ago, Abraham Maslow came up with an idea about a 'Hierarchy of Needs'. The interventions and strategies you introduce for yourself or others are more effective when they follow a continuum. Maslow believed that we must first satisfy our basic, biological needs before we can successfully address the higher, more 'cerebral' ones. In other words, I'm not so likely to find fulfillment painting or gaining skills on the balance beam if I am starving and in need of shelter. Woody Allen is sometimes quoted as saying, "Ninety percent of life is just showing up."[9] Feed me first, and give me proper shelter (biological needs); *then* I'll be more prepared to pursue self-actualization in other areas. If I weigh 400 pounds, and I have never worked out a day in my life, I need to consider my physical resources *at this time* when I come up with an exercise regimen. This, and the baseline component, practically targets the *abilities* section of the formula for change. I always endeavor to meet you where you *are*—not where you *should* be; I suggest that you do the same. Many clients start counseling with a 'crisis intervention' focus; with time, however, they usually get beyond that to address more 'enhancement' issues in their lives. Of course I will keep my 'eye on the prize' as the changes come about one day at a time. In the program of AA they say, "First Things First," meaning that Maslow's Hierarchy applies to everyone, everywhere. In considering this, **be certain to take care of the more basic, fundamental needs first** before you move up in your goals for change. Biological needs aside, such as proper nutrition, it may be fundamental for some individuals to educate themselves. Part of acquiring abilities may simply be initiated by *learning* how healthy couples argue, how to relax moderately, or getting coached about an appropriate exercise regimen. In all cases, take care of your body *first*, in whatever way that applies to you, before moving up the scale.

People in AA often bring up another one of their slogans in lieu of the alcoholic's propensity to make most things more involved, complex and extreme than is necessary: 'Keep It Simple.' When it comes to your change, it is important to apply Occams' Razor. William of Occam (or Ockham) was a medieval philosopher who was famous for creating the principle of *parsimony;* that is, it is wise to 'shave off' things that are not needed when considering understanding or changing something. In other words, one should not make more assumptions than the minimum needed. Don't pull out the elephant gun to shoot the mouse! In deciding on goals and strategies for change in your life, **come up with the most simple and easy intervention(s) that will get the job done.** It reminds me of the story about the young child, while sitting at the table one night, asking his parents, "where did I come from?' Mom and Dad looked at each other anxiously, not quite prepared for 'the sex talk.' Dad cleared his throat and began going into detail about sperm and eggs, and the process of conception. When he was finished with his in-depth biological explanation, he said, "Do you understand, now, all about where you came from?" Junior thought for a moment, a puzzled look on his face, and then responded, "Well, I thought I came from New Jersey!" KEEP IT SIMPLE—sometimes 'a cigar is just a cigar.'

Whether you are gaining skills in arguing well, identifying irrational self-talk, replacing and redefining anxious feelings with excitement, imagining yourself peaking in front of hundreds, losing weight and creating the strong, healthy body you want, replacing a destructive addiction with a healthy one, or acquiring any new habit, it should be 'standard operating procedure' to **become proficient at breathing.** Developing a slow, effective breathing technique, as I had mentioned previously in this book, is a key to gaining self control, calming down, breaking an automatic response, preparing your mind for a creative, new thought, and basically keeping 'Joe' in the basement.

Once you have conjured up a realistic goal for change, take a moment to relax, using the PMR technique previously described, and **imagine (visualize) yourself either completing the goal or at least successfully participating in it.** When you are physically relaxed, you are more open to suggestions, and frequently more amenable to creativity. For example, you could do a PMR exercise, then use your imagination to create a realistic picture of yourself at your ideal weight, arguing well, attaining an athletic goal, living free of depression or anxiety, speaking comfortably in front of others, completing an educational goal, being physically healthy, standing up for yourself with others, being a non-smoker, or *whatever* you decide (see chapter 8 for examples). The more clear and acceptable the image you have of succeeding, the better the prognosis. Just like the Russian weightlifters discovered, practice *seeing* yourself successfully arriving at whatever goal(s) you have set, and do it often until it becomes your reality. Even if you may have initial doubts about successfully achieving a goal, go through this process *anyway* and, if need be, *forcefully* create a scenario of success at whatever you have determined. If you find yourself slipping in to an old conditioned, automatic pattern of viewing yourself, simply stop the image (like a movie) and replace the scene with what you now desire for yourself-*regardless of how it feels.* You know that *Pain* and *Desire* must be part of the formula, even when you have acquired the necessary skills or abilities. When you expect pain and desire to be part of the 'cost' for change, you are more prepared to utilize them—and *change* happens!

Operationalize your goal(s); adhere to the definition of 'love'; develop it around the formula for happiness; create a realistic baseline from which to start; take care of more basic needs/goals first; use Occam's Razor; become proficient at breathing; develop powerful images, 'run your own race', but forcefully stick to images of success—*regardless of how it feels!*

11

Plugging It In

The goal of any good therapist is to put him/herself 'out of 'business' as soon as possible. When I have treated someone for awhile, I notice that, within a relatively short time, they can come to 'second guess' what I am about to say. After they become familiar with my cognitive strategies, and coaching, they begin to think, "What would Bob say?" They start to easily answer this and, with time, as they gradually become their own therapist, they find themselves thinking, "what would *I* say?' By simply reflecting upon what this book has taught you, it can guide you as you flow through the common sense process of change. Allow me to 'prime the pump' as you embark on your journey.

Imagine, if you would, that you are 'sick and tired of feeling sick and tired', and you

> **Get honest** *for a moment. Pretend that none of your excuses are legitimate anymore. Step out of yourself briefly and just see if you can imagine yourself really changing. What would it be like? What would you be thinking? What would it feel like? How do you think it would affect others around you? Is this really what you want? Now, honestly, write down if it is worth it to you. By this time you will know whether change is about to happen for you.*

finally decide to go for a few counseling sessions in order to 'address some issues'. Just as in any business decision, it is important to be an informed consumer. As in any other businesses, a referral by a satisfied customer is always the best way of finding an effective counselor. In addition, you should be comfortable when you speak with the potential therapist on the phone; and don't be afraid to ask questions about his /her training, experience, education, or anything you consider relevant to what may be your presenting problem—trust your guts. There are plenty of 'professionals' out there, with all kinds of credentials, who are ineffective, neurotic individuals who are, unfortunately, simply trying to work out their own problems through the clients they treat—be a smart consumer. Before you initiate your first session, briefly review what has led you to make the appointment. As I said earlier, nobody calls a therapist because they're having such a great day; it is *Pain* that led you to this decision, and, on some level, begin to acknowledge that pain is your friend—if you choose to use it. In your initial session I would ask you:"What is the presenting problem?" following the proper releases and HIPPA requirements.[10] Occasionally, people are not sure what their presenting problem is, and it may take a few sessions to narrow it down. On the other hand, I find it very helpful to conceive of things in the *positive* whenever possible, as we 'operationalize the goal(s); for example, **how would you know when treatment was a success?** If you wanted to, you could take a moment to answer this question now for yourself.

The next order of business in the initial session would be one of gathering some relevant history. How long have you had the problem (If it is *problem* focused) and what, if anything, have you done about it in the past? I would go over past treatment, if any, briefly reviewing both positive and negative outcome; and, remember, *specifics* are always better than generalities: With whom; for what; for how long; and when you did it, are all up for grabs. You certainly don't want to re-invent the wheel, but you also don't want to 'do the same thing over and over, expecting different results'. **If you have attempted to tackle this change goal in the past, what have you tried, and how did it work**

out for you? Learn from your success and failures of the past—they were hard earned lessons that constituted the first part of the formula for change, so don't just slough them off! What's different now? You could probably also answer this question right now if you take a few moments to think about it.

Always keep in mind during this process, the formulas for change, happiness, and the overriding definition of *love* as it applies to you or others, as the three most important guidelines in the proposed change(s) you are addressing (I certainly would).

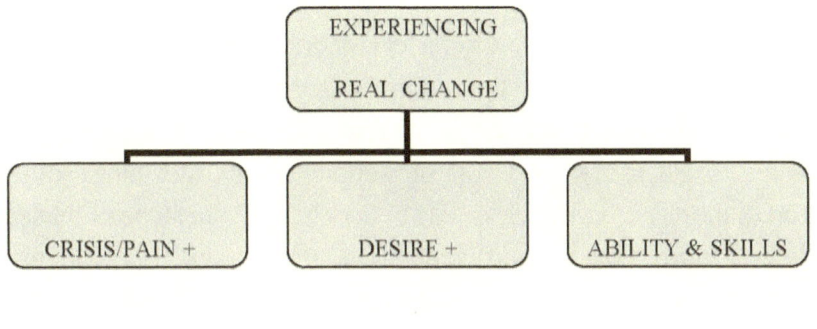

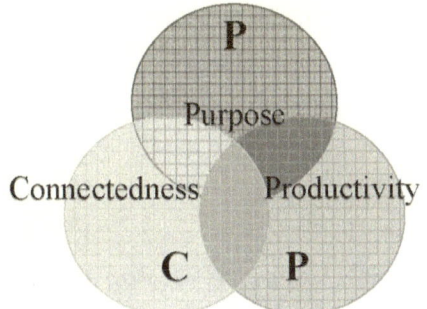

During the course of your first sessions the concept of values, *your values*, typically surfaces. Just what *are* your values, and how do they play into the change(s) you desire? Our myopic views can sell us short when we are formulating goals for change in our lives; that is, **in the big picture, what is it all for**; how does your life *Purpose* fit in here? This is well worth the thought and effort as, without this consideration, you could just be 'spinning your wheels' to bring about a change that, in the long run, isn't really worth the time and effort. For example, does getting sober 'fit in' with your future plans and your life goals? You might be surprised how this one issue cuts off a lot of the 'fat' relevant to worthy change goals, and brings to the surface some 'hidden agendas' with people. Perspective can be so important and so missing in our lives nowadays, and this gets to the heart of it.

How does your goal for change affect those around you, or play into your relationships with others (*Connectedness*)? **Remember that real change never occurs in a vacuum**. Even though you are ultimately responsible for yourself, you are not alone in this world (if you *are*, that has to be remedied). I would get a feel for your support system, or lack thereof, and the 'challenges' you may be facing relevant to your change goals and the people you surround yourself with. For example, if you wanted to get sober, what sort of 'people, places and things' do we need to modify or consider as part of the change? This type of thinking allows a more 'holistic' and workable approach; and it guarantees a better overall prognosis. How often have I seen a recovering alcoholic struggle through his/her first year of sobriety only to have the spouse help them 'celebrate' by buying a bottle of wine?! This, by the way, was the *same* spouse who had endlessly nagged about the problems drinking had caused! Among other things, *Connectedness* addresses the system that you live with when establishing change.

After I narrow down the presenting problem, defined in positive terms, and review the history of it, I would typically **go over a very brief history of your family** (especially looking at patterns that seem to repeat themselves). This isn't as difficult as it may seem, and it certainly doesn't take *years* of introspection. Remember, as I said previously, the goal is not to place any blame or accountability for your actions on family, but simply to get an overview of possible family patterns and dynamics and to give us a 'heads up' for possible hurdles you may be on the lookout for—it's very cost-effective in the 'big picture.' Just for fun, try assigning an adjective (one word description) to everyone in your immediate family.[11] Just remember, in order to get accurate directions, it helps to know how you got to your present location.

Following the establishment of your baseline, your current level of functioning, it would then be time to **proceed with weekly, tangible steps** leading you toward those change goals. Remember that 'all-or-nothing' (Dichotomous) thinking only sets you up for defeat. A little done a lot is always better than a lot done a little! Remember, you will 'act your way into feelings' not 'feel your way into actions' once we start the journey of change; and this precept fits very nicely into the aspect of *Productivity* here. During the course of therapy, I will also frequently take a moment to go back and review the original change goal(s) in order to assess progress and the relevance of the goals as you progress; sometimes things evolve as time goes by. Never be afraid to 'check in' from time to time. I find that this process frequently has the added benefit of fueling your ongoing *Desire.* When you get discouraged, it is often inspirational to take a step back and consider where you were a few months ago as compared to where you are now.

'**To the best of your ability, are you acting in a way that is** truly **the best interest of yourself and/or others'** when considering this change?' Keeping this guiding principle in the back of your mind throughout the entire process, you will afford yourself the foundation necessary for lasting change. If your change goal is to 'get back at every bastard who has ever hurt you', I might suggest that you consider modifying. I have had many potential clients requesting hypnosis to 'forget about an ex' or to 'make me not care anymore' about someone who is significant in their life. Such goals would ignore the formula for change. A' working through' process is necessary, in which *Pain, Desire* and *Ability* must interface in order to bring about legitimate, lasting change. In addition, any mind-numbing 'shortcut' would likely not be in your best interest; thus, the definition of *Love* would be sullied.

Now that you have 'cut the fat' off your change goal and transformed it into a workable, practical, balanced and healthy outcome, you are well on your way to tackling the *Ability* component of the formula. It is time to initiate 'first things first' considering Maslow's Hierarchy. I would begin to teach you how to **gain control of your body and mind as you embark.** In many presenting problems, learning how to become proficient at Progressive Muscle Relaxation (PMR) never hurts, and it usually helps to prepare your mind for the change(s) you desire (see chapter eight). If you have particular difficulty learning or implementing PMR, you might consider finding a massage therapist or a Biofeedback Therapist in order to help develop your skills.[12] This is also an excellent time, especially if you are changing depression or anxiety-related symptoms, to initiate an exercise program—regardless of how it feels. Start where you are *at.* Maybe 10-20 minutes a day of brisk walking suits your needs for now. Perhaps you are in better shape, and a regular aerobic routine is right up your alley; either way, this becomes the initiation of change for most presenting problems. If you want to get 'Freudian' on me, you can also view your willingness of starting an exercise regimen as a symbolic gesture that you are, in fact, 'ready' for change in your life. Either way, get your butt off the couch!

The A-B-Cs come into play at this juncture and I enjoy going over how the mind works, including a detailed explanation of the A-B-Cs during the first couple of sessions. It is usually pretty beneficial to tape-record this session so that you can review and become increasingly more proficient in your understanding of how your mind works. In addition, periodically reviewing the cognitive distortions (dysfunctional 'self-talk') enables you to get ever better at identifying them and replacing them in your life with realistic, functional self-talk.

Remember that your self-talk, on a sub-vocal level, is *constantly* percolating down into your subconscious whether you like it or not. Your self-talk will either lead to reasonable, manageable emotions, or, depending on how irrational and extreme you have been, may be the very source and solution to the emotional runaway train you have unwittingly created. The decision to take charge of your mind, as opposed to having it whimsically take charge of you, is now becoming a reality.

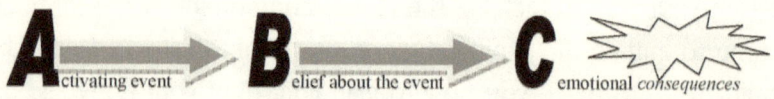

A—activating event (What starts the process) B—elief about the event (What you tell yourself/self-talk) C—emotional consequences (What you end up feeling)

Within a couple of sessions, most clients are already recognizing their often prolific use of irrational and distorted self-talk. Once you familiarize yourself with *Dichotomous Thinking* (black and white, absolutes), *Filtering* (letting in only the negative while 'filtering out the positive), *Catastrophizing* (using 'tweaked up' ,extreme words to describe things), and *Emotional Reasoning* (confusing thoughts with feelings, or letting 'Joe' define your reality), you can quickly begin to **identify and replace** them with more inclusive, reasonable and manageable self-talk. Don't be afraid to keep a journal; write down instances when you catch yourself using these distortions—and replace them. Within a short time, this inevitably leads to more reasonable and manageable emotions. Many clients are amazed at just how pervasive their cognitive distortions are, once they become 'coached' around their self-talk. I liken it to you living next to a train station. With time you probably habituate to the earthquake-like shaking and the constant rumbling of the trains to the extent of not even noticing it. Of course, when I come over to socialize, and the coffee glasses are being vibrated off the table, I might exclaim, "What the heck is *that*?!" Chances are, you would reply with, "…Oh, I hadn't noticed." The 'rumbling and shaking' caused by your constant use of distortions has definitely outlived its' usefulness—identifying and replacing them now starts to flow. Whether you accomplish this on your own, or with a 'coach', the process can easily take on a life of its' own, and change happens.

By now, I would enjoy periodically having you go through a relaxation exercise (PMR), maybe hooking you up to a biofeedback device, to see how you are progressing with the extent to which you are gaining relaxation skills. You can surely practice these skills on your own, and rate yourself as you enhance your ability to relax in various situations. In the event that you find yourself simply *stuck* on something traumatic from your past, and you just cannot get over it, you might consider finding a professional skilled in Eye Movement Desensitization and Reprocessing (EMDR).[13] I routinely utilize EMDR as it only takes a couple of sessions, and

I have found the results to be truly amazing.

During the course of learning to relax, you might find it easier to **gain increased mastery of slow, deep breathing, as it becomes essential during your changes.** Remember the footnote about the breathing training I mentioned in Chapter eight? My many years in the martial arts, experience as a Police Officer, practicing biofeedback, watching incredible feats performed by yoga instructors, have convinced me of the practicality of breath control. That slow-deep breath, prior to saying anything significant or acting on an emotion, can save you from those 'automatic' responses that, in the past, have caused so much trouble. Now is the time to put this to use. It creates that all-important moment that is necessary in breaking loose from the past actions and thoughts, and it gives you the opportunity to introduce the change you have worked so hard to achieve. Imagine taking that slow, deep breath prior to responding to something your spouse said that, in the past, would have caused you to 'flood'. You could have been reviewing the *eight rules* of good arguing (chapter six) and that breath might save you from slipping back into the same old rut. Joe the Custodian *hates* it when you incorporate the slow, deep breath into your routine of change.

Depending on the presenting problem, changing your mind may very well be accomplished by now. There are venues, however, that might be considered as reinforcement for these changes in your life. As a general rule, **the use of guided imagery can pay off in a big way at this point**. As I mentioned in Chapter eight, you can easily write out your own imagery script in order to address whatever change you desire. Take a moment to 'walk through' the change goal(s) incorporating as much detail, and as many senses as possible, and then simply write down your story of success, step-by-step, using the guidelines I gave you. Creating goal-oriented scripts, relapse-prevention, life enhancement, problem-solving or motivational imagery for yourself is only limited by your imagination—which is *unlimited!* Remember, *What the mind can conceive, the body can achieve.*

Any imagery script you decide to develop can be formatted by:

- Abiding by the guidelines I provided relevant to clearly formulating your change goals, in conjunction with the formulas for change, happiness, and the definition of love. Examples might be: *to eliminate depression and anxiety; to achieve a weight of____; to become a non-smoker; to enhance my relationship and communicate more effectively; to run the Boston marathon; to overcome my fear of___; to improve my parenting skills; to enhance my stress management skills,* etc.

- Utilizing all the senses whenever possible. 'Walk' through your scene describing fragrances, the feeling of the sun or the cool, gentle breeze on your skin. Describe, in detail, your emotions, what you see, what you hear—even what you may taste, if possible.

- Taking advantage of creativity by 'breaking the rules' if necessary. You can 'freeze-frame scenes, back-space, enlarge or minimize what you see. Step in to the image any way you like, and go beyond any temporal boundaries. Anything you can think of, you can imagine.

- Take frequent pauses whenever you like, and record your images using a monotone voice, considering having calming music or nature sounds in the background.

Following an effective relaxation exercise, depending on your change goal, you might come up with something such as this:

I see myself now walking along a path, deep in a beautiful forest. Birds sing in the distance, and the sweet smell of honeysuckle fills the air. The sun is filtering through the leaves of the trees as the branches rustle, dancing melodically to the gentle swing of the warm, summer breeze. I have been clean and sober now for over a year, and it feels good; it feels right. I am standing tall and confident as I walk, taking one step at a time. Rounding the bend I notice a table on my left, covered with an ornate embroidered cloth. I pause to examine it. There are various plates of delectable foods, the seductive fragrance of freshly cooked Italian bread and a large bottle of wine...my favorite wine, open and ready to be tasted. I stop, take a slow deep breath, aware of my pulse increasing, and the scene freezes. I turn to the right and suddenly become aware of someone standing next to me; it is me, the addict inside. He opens a door, and we walk through. I am transported to tomorrow, after I take that first drink. I am sick, filled with remorse. My wife and children are looking upon me in pregnant silence as they find me only now awakening on the living room floor, covered in vomit from the night before. I am overcome by that all too familiar self-loathing...and I cry. (Pause) The Woulda-Coulda-Shouldas rush in on me—but wait, I realize that I did not actually take that first drink yet! I rush back through the door to the forest path where the table and the wine remain untouched. Given another chance, I quickly run from the table, further down the path into a group of my friends from AA. They welcome me, embrace me, and once again I feel whole—ready for another day by the Grace of God! Create anything you want; write it all down, and record it—so much better than TV!

Change is possible when you follow the approach described in this book. Do not allow yourself to succumb to the 'self-fulfilled prophecy' of doing the same stupid things over and over, expecting different results. Be creative. Be open. Change your mind!

Appendix A

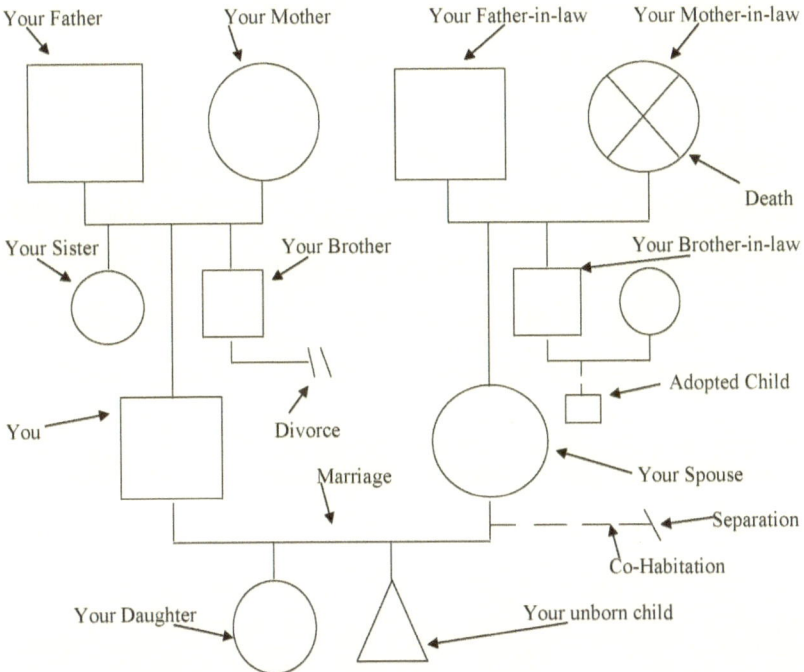

A typical Genogram uses similar symbols, usually covering three generations of your family, in which you can get an overview of patterns without a lengthy narrative. There are more symbols, such as a line around a family member who has been 'cut off', or a squiggly line between two members who do not get along. Remember, assigning an adjective for each member can give you a succinct 'feel' for what family members represent to you. It's amazing how many people suddenly 'see' patterns they never saw before when they complete a Genogram; but, as I said, this technique may be more amenable to professionals. As mentioned, we need not blame our family for our actions, but we can give ourselves a 'heads up' when we decide change is necessary. A quick family overview lets us become more aware of some possible support we have, or the 'challenges' we may face due to their influence.

"Biofeedback is a process that enables an individual to learn how to change physiological activity for the purposes of improving health and performance. Precise instruments measure physiological activity such as brainwaves, heart function, breathing, muscle activity, and skin temperature. These instruments rapidly and accurately "feed back" information to the user. The presentation of this information—often in conjunction with changes in thinking, emotions, and behavior—supports desired physiological changes. Over time, these changes can endure without continued use of an instrument.

Biofeedback is a non-invasive form of treatment. The therapist attaches sensors or electrodes to the body and these sensors provide a variety of readings--*feedback*--which is displayed on the equipment for the patient to see. The signals typically measure skin temperature, muscle tension and/or brainwave function. With this information, patients can learn to make changes so subtle that at first they cannot be consciously perceived. With practice, however, the new responses and behaviors can help to bring relief and improvement to a variety of disorders.

Through biofeedback a person experiencing migraines can learn to ward off headaches. A person who experienced a stroke may regain muscle use. Children and adults diagnosed with ADD or ADHD may see improved concentration and control. People with urinary or fecal incontinence or other pelvic floor disorders can achieve improved bladder control. Individuals with stress-related disorders learn to relax and improve their overall health."[15] (BCIA.org).

References

Ahsen, A. (1982) Imagery in perceptual learning and clinical application. *Journal of Mental Imagery, 6,*157-186.

Bellack, A.S., Glanz, M. & Simon, R. (1976) Self-reinforcement style and covert imagery in the treatment of obesity. *Journal of Consulting and Clinical Psychology, 44,* 490-491.

Bras, H., Lahjouji, F., Korogod, S.M., Kulagina, I.B. & Barbe, A. (2003) Heterogeneous synaptic covering and differential change transfer sensitivity among the dendrites of 9 reconstructed abducens motor neurone: Correlations between electron microscopic and computer simulation data. *Journal of Neurocytology. (Vol. 32),* Number 1, January, 5-24 (20).

Breggen, P.R. (2008) *Medication madness: A psychiatrist exposes the dangers of mood-altering medications.* New York: St. Martin's Press.

Colman, A.M. (2001) PET scan. *A dictionary of psychology.* December. http://www.encyclopedia.com.

Conges, J.J. (1988) Hostages to fortune: Youth, values, and the public interest. *American Psychologist, Vol. 43*(4), April, 291-300.

Cousins, N. (1979) *Anatomy of an illness.* New York: W.W. Norton.

Cousins, N. (1983) *The healing heart.* New York: W.W. Norton.

DeYoung, R., (2009). *A single-case design implementing eye-movement desensitization and reprocessing (EMDR) with an ex-cult member.* Professional paper presented at International Cultic Studies Association Annual Conference, Geneva, Switzerland; pending publication in the ICSA journal.

DeYoung, R. (2008) Bullet-proofing the mind: Applying SIT to law enforcement. *Law Officer,* March, 38-40.

DeYoung, R. (2009) Going tactical with EMDR: A state of the art intervention. *New York Tactical,* Spring; pending publication.

DeYoung, R. (1999) Investigative hypnosis: Faking, fallacy and facts. *The Forensic Examiner, (VoL.8),* January/February, 20-22.

Dossey, L. (1993) *Healing words: The power of prayer and the practice of medicine.* Harper: San Francisco.

Einstein, A., http://www.brainyquote.com/quotes/quotes/a/alberteins148799.html. *Einstein Quotes.* http://www.einstein-quotes.com/content/view/12/26/.

Ellis, A. (1993) Fundamentals of rational-emotive therapy for the 1990's. In Dryden & L.K.Hill (Eds.) *Innovations in rational emotive therapy.* New York: Sage. (pp.36-48).

Fanning, P. (1994) *Visualization for change.* Oakland, CA: New Harbinger.

Farah, M.J. (1984) The neurological basis of mental imagery: A componential analysis. *Cognition, 18,* 245-272.

Freeman, A., Simon, K.M., Arkowitz, H., & Beutler, L. (Eds.) (1989) *Handbook of cognitive therapy.* New York: Plenum Press.

Goldenberg, G., Mullbacher, W. & Nowak, A. (1995) Imagery without perception-A case study of anosognosia for cortical blindness. *Neuropsychologia, 33,* 1373-1382.

Heylighen, F. (1997) *Occam's Razor.* Principia Cybernetica Web.

Hull, A.M. (2002) Neuroimaging findings in post-traumatic stress disorder. *The British Journal of Psychiatry, 181,* 102-110.

Jorgensen, C. (2004) http://www.nasa.gov/centers/ames/news/releases/2004/subvocal/subvocal.html

Kaye, S.M. & Robert, M. (2001) *On Ockham.* Belmont: Wadsworth.

Kennedy, S.H., Konarski, J.Z., Segal, Z.V., Lau, M.A., Beiling, P.J., McIntyre, R.S. & Mayberg, H.S. (2007) Differences in brain glucose metabolism between responders to CBT and venlafaxine in a 16 week randomized control trial. *American Journal of Psychiatry.* May, 164, 778-788.

Kirk, C.C. & Griffey, D.C. (1995-96) The effects of imagery and language cognitive strategies on dietary intake, weight loss, and perception of food. *Imagination, Cognition and Personality, 15,*145-157.

Kosslyn, S.M., Behrmann, M. & Jeannerod, M. (1995) The cognitive neuroscience of mental imagery. *Neuropsychologia, 33,* 1335-1344.

Mayberg, H. (2005) Positron emission tomography imaging in depression: A neural systems perspective. *Neuroimaging Clinics of North America, (Vol. 13),* Issue 4, 805-815.

Lamb, M.E., Bornstein, D. & Teti, D.M. (2002) *Development in infancy: An introduction.* Mahwah, N.J.: Lawrence Erlbaum Associates.

Maslow, A.H. (1970) *Motivation and personality.* New York: Harper & Row.

Maslow, A.H. (1971) *The farther reaches of human nature.* New York: Viking.

McGoldrick, M., Gerson, R., & Shellenberger, S. (1999). *Genograms: Assessment and intervention.* New York: W.W. Norton.

Premack, D. (1983) Animal cognition. *Annual Review of Psychology, 34, 351*-362.

Premack, D. & Premack, A.J. (1983) *The mind of an ape.* New York, Norton.

Shapiro, F. (2002). EMDR 12 years after its introduction: Past and future research. *Journal of Clinical Psychology, 58* (I), 1-22. doi:10.1002/jclp.1126.

Shapiro, F., & Forrest, M. S. (2004). *EMDR: The breakthrough therapy for overcoming anxiety, stress and trauma* (Rev. ed.). New York, NY: Basic Books.

Sheik, A.A. (2003) *Healing images: The role of imagination in health.* Amityville, NY: Baywood Publishing.

Stevick, R.A. (2007) *Growing up Amish.* Baltimore, Johns Hopkins University Press.

Wickramasekera, I.E., (1998) *Clinical behavioral medicine: Some concepts and procedures.* New York, Plenum Press.

Endnotes

[1] 12-step programs, usually modeled after Alcoholics Anonymous (AA), come in many forms, and typically address addictions such as gambling, sex, over-eating, spending, narcotics, etc. They rest on anonymity and involve a self-help format in which the members base their 'recovery' on systematically working through a hierarchy of twelve principles (steps). Participants can turn things around, in part, by sharing their 'experience, strength and hope'. Father Martin, one of the 'old-timers' of AA, summarized the first three steps as, "I can't do it; God can; I think I'll let Him."

[2] Much of the material I am going to present here was originated by the late Dr. Albert Ellis, the developer of Rational Emotive Behavior Therapy (REBT). I would also like to give credit to my mentor at Philadelphia College of Osteopathic Medicine, Dr. Art Freeman, one of the most prolific Cognitive Behavior Therapists in America.

[3] As custodial work is an honorable profession and, hopefully, custodians read self-help books too, I mean no disrespect by the analogy.

[4] Dr Ellis provides many more distortions, as examples, but I find the one's provided here are the most common.

[5] The Premack principle postulates that any high frequency response can be used to reinforce a low frequency response; in other words, observing what someone spends time doing when

they have free time, will allow you to find out what is reinforcing to that person.

[6] Placing a five pound weight on your stomach, such as a book, while lying down can serve as a training tool; practice having your stomach lift the book with each breath, and then lowering it down as you exhale, without moving your chest; this will develop a 'muscle memory' for proper breathing technique.

[7] This technique is frequently used in forensic hypnosis to facilitate recall of important events or facts.

[8] If you are unable to 'see' a particular image, you can simply 'cut and paste' whatever you would like, and transpose it on yourself. Some people may also find 'feeling-oriented' (Tactile) scenarios work better for them.

[9] According to WordPress.com, however, he actually said," Eighty percent of success is showing up." I prefer the first rendition.

[10] The 'Health Information Portability and Privacy Act (HIPPA) guarantees your privacy, as well as other relevant legal and ethical concerns in counseling.

[11] If you *really* feel industrious, you could make up a *Genogram,* which is a diagrammatic representation of your family (a therapeutic 'family tree'), but that may be more suited for a professional at this point. (see appendix A).

[12] The Biofeedback Certification Institute of America (BCIA) is the largest and most recognized professional certifying organization for Biofeedback, and is an excellent source for additional information. BCIA.org.(see Appendix B).

[13] Francine Shapiro, the developer of EMDR, published her first journal article in 1989, and the technique has since grown to

become an almost standard intervention for trauma treatment. See www.emdr.com for more information.

[14] Is this the part when I say, "Joe sent me?"

[15] This entire page description was taken from the definition adopted by BCIA , AAPB and ISNR as of 5/18/08.See BCIA.org. Photo courtesy of Naomi DeYoung.

www.ingramcontent.com/pod-product-compliance
Lightning Source LLC
Chambersburg PA
CBHW020251290526
45784CB00003B/1204